Hutchinson Checkbook Se...

Oral Work

Roy Blatchford and Melvyn Elphee

Series Editor
Roy Blatchford

Hutchinson

London Melbourne Sydney Auckland Johannesburg

Other titles in the series

Comprehension Bill Deller and Michael Taylor
Literature Roger Lewis, Gill Pugmire and Martin Pugmire
Punctuation Philip Payne
Spelling Martin Tucker
Summary Ken Methold and Roy Blatchford
Writing Linda Cookson

Hutchinson Education

An imprint of Century Hutchinson Ltd,
62-65 Chandos Place, London WC2N 4NW

Century Hutchinson Australia Pty Ltd
PO Box 496, 16-22 Church Street, Hawthorn, Victoria
3122, Australia

Century Hutchinson New Zealand Limited
PO Box 40-086, Glenfield, Auckland 10, New Zealand

Century Hutchinson South Africa (Pty) Limited
PO Box 337, Bergvlei 2012, South Africa

First published 1986
Reprinted 1987

© Roy Blatchford and Melvyn Elphee 1986

Set in 11/12pt Century Schoolbook
by D. P. Media Limited, Hitchin, Hertfordshire

Printed and bound in Great Britain by Anchor Brendon
Limited, Tiptree, Essex

British Library Cataloguing in Publication Data
Blatchford, Roy
    Oral work. — (Hutchindon checkbooks series)
    1. Oral communications — Study and teaching
    (Secondary) — Great Britain
    I. Title   II. Elphee, Melvyn
    001.54′2′071241   P95.4.G7

ISBN 0 09 159521−5

Contents

Introduction

A book on oral work is something of a contradiction! Whereas punctuation, essay writing, comprehension, spelling all happen in book form, oral communication does not. Therefore this book can only come to life in the mouths, ears and brains of its users. Just as a good play *needs* its audience, so this book *needs* its readers. More than in the other *Checkbooks*, you, the student, are necessarily part of the book.

Note for the teacher

Some of the activities can be done with the whole class, a few by the student alone, but most need small groups or pairs.

Many of the exercises can be adapted easily for follow-up written work.

Acknowledgments

The Publishers' thanks are due to the following for permission to reproduce copyright material:

Edward Arnold *(Publishers)* Ltd for Maps B and C, taken from *Mapwork* by Dena Procter *('Foundation Geography'* series); the author for extracts from *A Likely Lad* by Gillian Avery (published *Collins* 1971); Guardian Newspapers Ltd for article by Lydia Kemeny *(The Guardian,* 6th September 1979); the estate of the late Sonia Brownell Orwell and Secker and Warburg Ltd for extract from *The Road to Wigan Pier* by George Orwell; London Regional Transport for Map A; John Murray Ltd for extract from *Summoned by Bells* by Sir John Betjeman; *She* magazine for article on *'Parents' Evenings'* by Alison Edwards; Welsh Joint Education Committee for passage and questions on *'The wig department at the Royal Opera House, Covent Garden';* the author for *'I must go down to the sea again'* by Spike Milligan and Gervasse Phinn for role plays.

Talking

A Why do we talk?

Sometimes we talk because we have something to say—but not very often! Mostly we talk just to show that we're friendly. Think of the stupid conversations people have at parties or on buses: it's not what they say that matters, it's the mere fact of their talking. And do you know the feeling of panic when one of those sudden silences descends? Often our closest friends are not only people we find it easy to talk to but, more importantly, people we find it easy to be silent with.

Perhaps it is because we are aware that we 'talk a load of rubbish' (or afraid that people may think we do) that many of us are very shy about talking at all, except with our closest friends. Slang phrases like 'rabbiting on' or 'gas bag' increase this feeling that we shouldn't talk too much. But just as good writers *can* write a lot, even though they may choose to make their points in a few words, so good talkers must have the *freedom* to talk as much as they like, even if they choose to weigh their words carefully.

So the first need in oral work is to fight shyness, embarrassment and self-consciousness—all of which hinder free talk.

Practice

1 **Warm-up** (*In pairs or larger groups up to class size*)

Take the initials of the people in the class and turn them into unusual hobbies and exotic foods. For example:

Name	Hobbies	Food
Alan Avis	Awful animals	Aniseed avocados
Peter Brown	Picking bluebells	Pickled blackberries
Janice Churcher	Jumping canals	Jugged cowslips
Anne Deacon	'Aving dreams(!)	Acorn dressing
Susan Fry	Sailing frisbees	Sausage fool

2 **Lists** (*Groups of 4 or more*)

The object is for each person to take it in turns to name in one minute as many items as they can from a given category. For example:

Category: clothes
Items: tie, handkerchief, scarf, socks, vest, shirt, skirt. . . . You are 'out' if you repeat a word, hesitate for more than five seconds (you can shorten the time as you get better) or put in an irrelevant item (e.g., in the category 'Clothes', the item 'lipstick' would be irrelevant).

Student **A** is the speaker.
Student **B** counts the number of words achieved and listens for repetition.
Student **C** times the minute and listens for hesitation.
Student **D** listens for irrelevance.

Discuss any disagreements about judgements. The person responsible for an area has a final vote should it be needed.

Rotate speaker and judges. This also develops LISTENING skills. The winner is the contestant with most words.

3 **Word tennis** (*Groups of 5 or more*)
As above, a category is given, but now there are two contestants. Each takes it in turn to say words from the category, again avoiding repetition, hesitation, irrelevance. When one runs out of words, the other wins a point.

A harder variation is to make the game follow an alphabetical pattern, so that the last letter of one word has to become the first letter of the next. For example:

Category: animals
Words: CaT, TigeR, RhinoceroS, SquirreL, LeoparD, DeeR, RaT. . . . Much harder—so allow a longer hesitation time.

4 **Gibberish** (*Pair work*)
Talk to each other *at the same time* for one minute. Then each try to tell the other what you think they were talking about. A very good exercise for building up CONCENTRATION.

5 **Word by word story** (*Groups of 2–6*)
Each person takes it in turn to contribute a word at a time to a story.

For example:

Once . . . there . . . were . . . three . . . rhinoceroses . . . who . . . lived . . . in . . . an . . . igloo . . . in . . . the . . . South . . . of . . . England . . . One . . . day . . .

6 **Sentence by sentence story** (*Groups of 2–6*)
As above, but a sentence at a time. More creative, but more demanding! Both these exercises also develop the concentration necessary for good listening skills. They can be done over and over again with different people, using different subjects.

B Something to say

Even if we talk most of the time just to be friendly, 'interesting' talk does have something to say.

COMMUNICATION = THOUGHT + EXPRESSION + UNDER-STANDING

ORAL COMMUNICATION = THOUGHT + TALK + LISTENING + UNDERSTANDING

No communication can get very far without *thought*. What goes on inside our heads is crucial to what comes out of our mouths.

On the other hand, we'd never have anything to say if we just sat around thinking impressive thoughts!

'How do I know what I think till I've said it?' is a piece of nonsense many of us have found to be true. So here are some ideas to get you talking—and the thinking will follow.

Practice

1 **Fortunately/unfortunately** (*Odd-numbered groups of 3, 5 or 7. Five is best.*)
Each person contributes a sentence to a story. Each sentence (except the first) must begin with 'Fortunately' and 'Unfortunately' alternately. No ideas or phrases should be repeated. For example:

John was late for school. Fortunately he had a good excuse. Unfortunately he had used it before. Fortunately his teacher was late too. Unfortunately the headmaster called the register. Fortunately he didn't know the class. . . .

2 **Yes, but . . .** (*Groups of 2 or more*)
This makes you think about ideas and develop them.

The first person makes a statement of opinion. Each person then continues with a sentence beginning 'Yes, but . . .'. For example:

—Smoking is bad for your health.
—Yes, but some people need a smoke to calm their nerves.
—Yes, but smoking can't get rid of your worries.
—Yes, but it can make them seem less important.
—Yes, but perhaps they *are* important.
—Yes, but nothing's important enough to get you down.
—Yes, but if you smoke and get ill, it'll get you down even more.
—Yes, but I'd rather be happy now than spend all my life trying to be healthy when I'm old. . . .

3 **'Tell me about the . . .'** (*Pairs*)
Student **A** says, 'Tell me about the . . .' and then chooses a word or phrase. For example: 'Tell me about the party'; 'Tell me about the shopping centre'; 'Tell me about the ghost'; 'Tell me about the lesser-spotted tree dolphin'.

Student **B** then has to talk for about a minute on the chosen subject as fluently as he/she can, keeping the first student's interest. Then swap roles.

4 **'Never mind that'** (*Pairs*)
A variation of 'Tell me about the . . .' which gives a more active role to the first partner and keeps the second on his or her toes.

Begin as in 'Tell me about the . . .', but as the story develops, the first student can interrupt to ask for more information about something just mentioned. This can happen any number of times at short or widely spaced intervals and the talker has to start immediately on the new topic. For example:

Student **A**: Tell me about the cat.
Student **B**: The cat clawed its way though the dark alley, ripping at the rags and prowling around dustbins. As he. . . .

Student **A**: Never mind that. Tell me about the dustbins.

Student **B**: The dustbins clattered. They were metal with plastic lids. Some of the lids were removed so that the cat could get inside and pull out chicken bones or dinner scraps. The stench. . . .

Student **A**: Never mind that, tell me about the chicken bones.

Student **B**: There were big bones, small bones, bones with meat on, bones that were almost chewed away. The cat tore at them hungrily, his great fangs ripping away the last vestiges of flesh. When he had eaten his fill he made his way past the shed, through the garden to the back door.

Student **A**: Never mind that, tell me about the garden.

Student **B**: The garden had a green lawn. . . .

Practice

Talking to the class

Here are some similar games to get you used to doing the same kind of thing in front of more people.

1 **Who am I?**
   Describe yourself to the class. (Can be practised first in pairs.)

2 **Who's who?**
   Say something to the class in half a minute about other members of the group.

3 **Lost something?**
   Arrive at a police station. Describe a lost object in half a minute.

4 **Guess what?**
   Describe an object without naming it. The class has to guess what it is.

5 **Likes and dislikes**
   Speak for a minute on why you like/dislike something intensely.

6 **Hat?**
   You each write your name and a subject on two pieces of paper.

The chairperson places them all in a hat.
You each select a name and pair it with a topic.
That person has to speak on that subject without hesitation, deviation, or repetition for one minute.
This can be timed and played on an elimination basis.

7 **Objects**
An object is placed under a cloth.
Each person has to feel it, then describe what he/she feels.
Others guess what it is from the description.
The teacher (or someone appointed) chairs by knowing the objects in advance.

8 **Excuses** (*Pairs*)
a) **The cheese game**
The customer (student **A**) must ask for several different kinds of cheese (one at a time). Each time the shopkeeper (student **B**) must give a different excuse as to why he or she doesn't have any. The winners are those who do not repeat a brand or an excuse. This can be adapted to a car showroom, an off-licence, a book-shop, a record shop or a sweet shop.

b) **The butler game**
The butler (student **A**) has just murdered the master of the house by shooting him with his own gun—the drawer is still open. Suddenly, the door bell rings. The lady of the house (student **B**) has arrived home early. The butler drags the corpse into the cellar and stuffs it in the freezer. He opens the door to the lady of the house, who demands to know why he kept her waiting. Just then she sees a dark red stain on the carpet. . . .
The butler must explain himself and try to prevent her following the drops down the stairs and opening the freezer lid.

Exercises and games develop confidence, fluency, concentration and quick-thinking.

Now it's time to put these to a more serious purpose—to express *yourself*.

• Either as a class or in small groups, see what you can find to say on each of the following subjects.

It is important that everybody has a say: have a speaker's chair and take it in turns to sit on the chair and say your piece. Even in small groups, each person should take it in turn to have their say before a more general discussion follows.

Subjects for discussion

Hobbies
Family
My favourite food
A person I'd like to meet
  and why
My favourite television
  programme and why
What makes me angry
If I ruled the world
What's wrong with school
My most embarrassing
  experience

If I had £1000
Where I'd like to live
The job I'd like
My favourite subject
Good points about me
Bad points about me
Phobias
Love is . . .
The sort of boy/girl I find
  attractive
School uniform
Exams

C Who are you talking to?

Now that you've had plenty of practice in saying what you want to say, it's time to think about the person (or people) you're saying it to. What do *they* want to hear?

In the sections that follow, you will practise the main purposes of spoken communication:

—reporting;
—instructing;
—explaining;
—describing;

—not just because you want or need to do it (though sometimes that's a good enough reason) but also because someone wants or needs to hear what you have to say.

—'What happened at the disco?'
—'Can you tell me how to make a cake?'
—'Why did you miss the last bus home?'
—'What was she wearing?'
—'Did you see the accident? What happened?'

These are the kinds of question people are always wanting us to answer—sometimes just for gossip, but sometimes as a really important matter of life and death. You *need* to be able to come up with the answers!

Here are some common situations we encounter in oral communication and some tips in dealing with them:

How to get there

When someone stops you in the street and asks you the way you have to:

—think quickly first;
—select relevant information;
—express it briefly and clearly in a good order.

Compare these:

Q: How do I get to the railway station?
A: You go down this road. At the end you turn left. When you get to the bridge you turn left just before it. There's some traffic lights first. Then you take the next turning on the left and you're there.

Was that clear? No! *Think first*. Put things in order. For example:

You go down to the end of this road, then turn left on to the main road. Carry on along it for about half a mile and you pass three sets of traffic lights. After the third set, take the next turning on the left, just before the bridge. It's called Station Road. The station is just in front of you—you can see it as soon as you turn into Station Road.

The same information—but this time it was *sorted* out in *order*.

Checklist

If you are asked to give directions you need to:

Visualize where you are now and where the person needs to get to.

Work out the shortest/best route.

If it's a motorist, remember where one-way streets are.

If you're not sure, say so!

Be clear in your mind.

Begin at the beginning.

Keep instructions simple (one step at a time).

Refer to street names and prominent landmarks (e.g., buildings).

Get left and right correct. Most people can follow these more easily than north and south, east and west, and they're more accurate than 'up' and 'down'.

Practice

1   (*Pairs*)

A speaks instructions. **B** draws a simple map, following **A**'s instructions. Swap roles after each question.

a) How do you get from this classroom to the staff room/the gym/the art rooms?

b) How do you get from the school/college gates to the nearest Post Office/pub/library/bus stop?

c) How do you get from home to the local disco/bus stop/ nearest cinema?

How often did you have to change an instruction or make it more precise for the map drawer to get it right? Could the map drawer offer any suggestions for improved instructions?

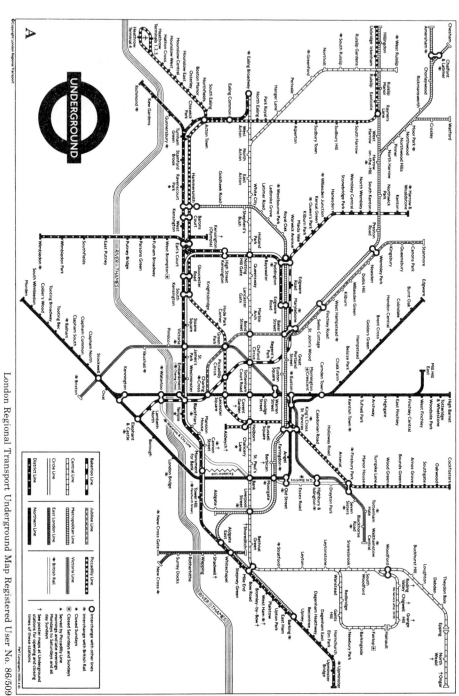

2   Look at map A. Take it in turns to ask and answer questions.

   a) How would you get from Watford Junction to Wimbledon?
   b) How do you get from Paddington to Waterloo?
   c) How do you get from Brixton to West Ruislip?
   d) How do you get from Camden Town to Kew Gardens?

   After each answer, the person who answered asks the questioner:

   —Was the answer audible?
   —Were the instructions clear?
   —Were they in the best order?
   —Was anything missed out?
   —Was there a better route?

   Carry on, each taking it in turn to make up your own question.

3   Now try a similar exercise using the more difficult map, B. Each take it in turn to make up a question.

4   Using map B, sit with a partner so that you can hear each other but can't see each other's map. One of you chooses a finishing point, but doesn't tell your partner where it is. Now give him/her a starting point and then all the directions to get to your finishing point. He/she follows the route with a pencil. Where does he/she end up?

5   Look at map C. One of you try describing a route to take your partner from one town to another. Name the starting point, but do not tell your partner which town you intend to direct him/her to. Both students look at their copies of the map. If instructions are carefully given and followed, the follower should end up in the finishing place the director thought of. If not, something is wrong with the instructions or the listening or both. Keep practising until you get it right. Change roles.

6   Still using map C, try these questions.

   a) How do you get from Byworth to Chipton?
   b) How do you get from Thorpe House to Silford?
   c) How do you get from Chipton to South Newton?

   Continue with your own examples until practice has made you clear, confident and quick.

B

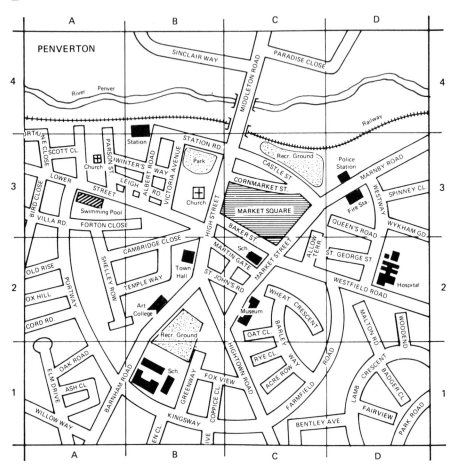

C

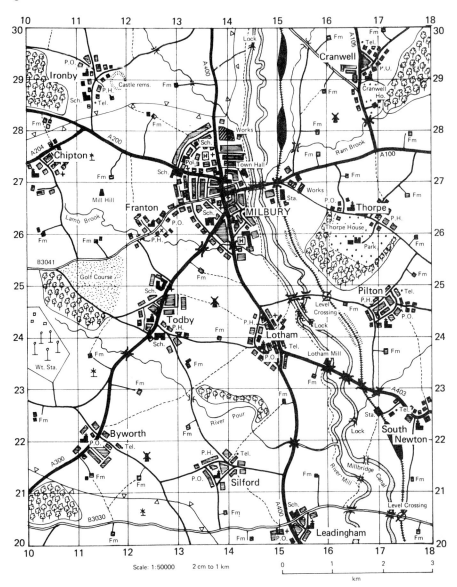

Scale: 1:50000   2 cm to 1 km

0   1   2   3

km

D How to do it

We spend a lot of our time asking or answering questions like these:

—How do I change a plug?
—How do I mend a puncture?
—How do I make a cake?
—How do I change a nappy?
—How do I make arrangements for a wedding?
—How do I work the washing machine?

If the answers are unclear we could be in trouble—often of a dangerous kind!

Look at this answer to the question, 'How do I make an omelette?'

'Break the egg. Add some milk, salt and pepper. Put it in a basin. Beat well. Turn into a frying pan. Heat it till it's cooked. Then slide it on to a plate. Delicious!'

Practice

1 What's wrong with that? Work it out for yourself, then check your answer against ours.

2 Can you give better instructions for making an omelette? Check your answer against ours.

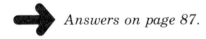 *Answers on page 87.*

Of course, it's quite hard to give instructions off the cuff—though that's usually how we have to do it. A few notes can help. Keep them clear, simple and well organized.

3 Explain each of the following without notes, then take five minutes to make brief notes and do the explanation again.

Don't write out a 'speech' in full—it will take a long time and will not sound natural and interesting to your hearers. So it is important to be able to give instructions from *notes*. But to do this you need to think through the speech.

 You will find a 'model answer' for the first one on page 88.

a) How to clean your teeth.
b) How to tie a tie.
c) How to play soccer/tennis—choose your own sport.
d) How to change the oil of the car.
e) How to play an instrument.
f) How to get a part-time job.
g) How to find a library book.

These can be done in pairs or as a whole class activity. If you're working in pairs, choose a topic each, both explain 'without notes', then take time to make notes and take it in turns to explain 'with notes'. In the whole class, random people may be chosen to talk spontaneously (without notes) on each of the topics. Then everyone can be given time for note preparation and different people chosen for the second versions.

E What did you see?

Describing people or incidents accurately can be of crucial importance—especially in road accidents or court cases.

Look at this part of a witness's description of a 'criminal':

—'He was wearing a blue jumper.'

Now look at the questions the defence asked.

—'Did it have sleeves?'
—'What sort of neck did it have?'
—'Were the sleeves rolled up?'
—'What style was it?'
—'Were there any stains or marks on it?'

By such questions the defence eventually succeeded in establishing that there were two men in blue jumpers and that the crime witnessed by the person giving evidence could not have been committed by her client. Careful observation and accurate description saved an innocent man from the verdict of 'guilty'.

Practice

1 (*In pairs*)
Describe someone in the classroom. Don't say who it is. Your partner must ask further questions to clarify accurate details about the person until he/she can identify him/her.

Change roles.

2 **Description game** (*pairs or whole class*)
Everyone draws a simple abstract shape, such as these.

They then have to get another person to draw their shape simply ·by giving precise spoken instructions and correcting them each time they go wrong. This can be done on the blackboard as a whole class activity or on paper in pairs.

3 A more difficult version of the 'Description game' requires the instructor to have his/her back to the artist so that he/she cannot see the effect of his/her instructions until the end. This gives scope for discussion of where things go wrong and is a situation parallel to giving instructions over the phone.

F Saying the right thing

What we say in one situation might not do very well in another. Do you speak in the same way to your best friends, your parents, your headteacher, your employer, your younger brother or sister? Saying the *right* thing in the *right* situation is a skill which most of us learn only gradually. We can probably all think of times when we have said the *wrong* thing at the *wrong* time! It is important in our everyday lives that we judge the mood of a room we walk into or the attitudes of people we meet if we are not to upset or confuse our listeners.

Practice

1 (*In pairs*)

You have just completed a journey by rail. As you walk along the platform to the barrier, you realize that you have lost your ticket. Improvise the dialogue between yourself and the ticket collector.

First of all, make it so that both characters are tactless and unhelpful.

Then do a second improvisation in which both are co-operative.

Finally—and this is more difficult—try it with the traveller polite and tactful, but the ticket collector uncooperative; then the other way round.

2 Now try three of the following situations, varying the characters to make them as real and interesting as you can.

Do each sketch three times:
First, with both characters uncooperative.
Then with both co-operative.
Finally, with one co-operative and the other not.

a) You set up camp one night and decide to pitch your tent in what seems to be a field. It is so dark that you can't see. In the morning you wake up to find that you have pitched camp on the lawn of a stately home. The owner is walking towards you. . . .

b) You have booked to stay in a very expensive hotel in the north of Spain. You arrive to find you have been moved to a less luxurious place several miles away. You meet up with the tour operator to demand your original rooms, but these have been let to someone else. . . .

c) You have decided to have a conversion done in your house. The builders start work. When you come home from work you see that they have knocked down the *wrong* wall! You point out the architect's drawings. . . .

d) You go to the hairdresser for a new-look style. Unfortunately your hair doesn't turn out the way you were promised it would by the hairdresser. . . .

e) You have borrowed some rare records from a friend. They are very valuable to her. She keeps reminding you that she wants them back. You say that you are still busy taping them, when in fact you have badly damaged them. Finally, she arrives on your doorstep wanting them returned. . . .

f) You and a friend are travelling on your motorbike. Your friend is not wearing a helmet. You are stopped by the police. . . .

3 Discuss *how* you felt as you played the different types of people. What sorts of behaviour produced the best results?

Some advice

If you want someone to do something for you, be pleasant to them.

If you want someone to be nice to you, be nice to them.

Anger produces anger.

Being reasonable produces a reasonable response.

G Interviews

Interviewer = person asking the questions
Interviewee = person being interviewed

It is worthwhile gaining experience as an interviewer as well as an interviewee. You will find it gives you a good insight into what people want when they ask questions and helps you to understand the shared responsibility of interviewer and interviewee in making a successful interview. As an interviewer you will easily recognize the shortcomings of those you interview: when it is your turn to be interviewed, you will find you are less likely to fall into the same pitfalls

What makes a good interview?

Look at the following:

Interviewer: How do you account for your sudden great success?
Pop star: Dunno, really.
Interviewer: Do you think it's because of your colourful stage-shows?
Pop star: Yeh, could be.
Interviewer: And what about those great video productions?
Pop star: Yeh, they were fun.

This interview is not successful because the interviewer has not obtained any real information. The pop star doesn't help!

Checklist

The ingredients for a successful interview are:

1 Questions which will lead to informative answers.

2 Short questions—it's the replies we're interested in.

3 Replies which are several sentences long so that we can learn something.

Asking questions

There are three types of question—closed questions, open questions and leading questions.

A closed question needs only a 'Yes' or 'No' answer, e.g. 'Do you like dogs?'

An open question allows for a fuller answer, going beyond yes or no, e.g. 'What do you think of dogs?'

A leading question hints at the answer you're expected to give, e.g. 'Don't you think dogs are lovely?'; 'Dogs are awful, aren't they?'

When *asking* questions try to ask as many open questions as possible and avoid closed and leading questions.

When *answering* questions, try to take the opportunities of the open question to give open, extended answers—not short, under-developed answers. For example:

Q: 'What do you think of dogs?'
A: 'Not much.'

This closes the open question and makes the questioner work too hard. A better approach would be:

Q: 'What do you think of dogs?'
A: 'I like big dogs, but I'm not very keen on poodles, dachsunds and small dogs in general. And I don't like to see dogs pampered. . . .'

This is an open answer which paves the way for a proper conversation. Closed questions and closed answers lead to stilted, dull conversations and poor interviews.

Here are some more examples of closed, open and leading questions:

Closed
1   Do you think there is enough pop music on TV?
2   Do you think the school-leaving age should be raised?
3   Do you like chocolates?

Open
1   What do you think of the amount of TV time given to pop music?
2   What's your opinion of the school-leaving age being raised?
3   What sorts of chocolates do you like best?

Leading
1   Shouldn't there be more pop music on TV?
2   Don't you think the school-leaving age should be raised?
3   Wouldn't you agree that chocolates are sickly?

Make up some more questions of the three different kinds and try them out on a partner.

Practice

1   In pairs, work out interviews based on the following situations.
    One person works on questions, the other on answers.

    An accident   Winning the pools
    A hobby   A daring rescue
    Record-breaking   Gaining a pay rise after a long
                              strike
    Winning a contest   Taking part in a national event

2   In pairs, work out interviews with the following as the person
    being interviewed:

    A politician   Handicapped person   Racing driver
    Film star   Sporting personality Drug addict
    Police chief/constable Headteacher   Author
    Pop singer   Jockey   Nurse

    The interview might be about the person's life (this would need
    some prior research) or it might be a quick interview following
    on a particualr incident in which the interviewee had been
    involved.

3   Conduct a *Desert Island Discs* session.
    In this radio programme a famous person is 'cast away' on a
    desert island. He/she has to choose the eight records he/she
    would take and say why. During the course of the programme
    the interviewer asks the person about his/her life and achieve-
    ments.

    This can be done 'live' or as a prepared tape recording. The
    interviewee can either be him/herself or act the role of someone
    famous.

    Variations: Favourite books, favourite people from history,
    favourite living people.

4   *This is Your Life*
    This could involve real or imagined people. The whole class can
    be actively involved, with someone doing the interview, one
    person as the subject and others as friends, colleagues, family.

H Being interviewed

The examiner should conduct a conversation with the candidate on other matters likely to be of interest to the candidate. The examiner's contribution should allow the candidate to demonstrate an ability to speak continuously, to explain and develop an idea and relate it to other ideas, and to handle objections and alternative points of view.

(London Regional Examinations Board)

A good starting point in the individual examination interview is the reading passage. If you are choosing your own, make sure you can talk about the book from which it is taken. (See page 54).

But what is really interesting to an interviewer is *you*. Don't worry if you don't have facts and knowledge at your fingertips. The interviewer is interested in your ability to project *yourself*. The best way to do this is to talk about yourself and the things you're interested in.

Practice

'What have you enjoyed/not enjoyed about school/college this year?'
'What's your favourite way of spending time?'
'What really annoys you and why?'
'Who is the most interesting person in your family?'

1 Write down four more questions you would like to ask a partner. First try answering them yourself. Were some questions hard to answer? Make them easier. Now ask your partner.

2 Prepare notes on these topics:

   My interests   My family
   My jobs   My friends
   My school/college   What I do at the weekends

3 Interview each other on these subjects. The interviewer should discuss the interviewee's performance on each of the points in the following Checklist:

Checklist

Remember: first impressions count for a lot.

Check: Appearance
         Manner
         Attitude
         Clarity

During the interview:
         Listen to the *end* of the question. Don't butt in.
         Don't answer in single words.
         Develop ideas.
         Talk *with* rather than *to* the examiner/interviewer.
         Engage his/her enthusiasm by demonstrating your own.
         Sound interested in your topic.
         Be aware of different viewpoints.

I Interviews for jobs

Once again, the interviewer will form an impression of you from your:

—Appearance
—Manner
—Speech
—Movements
—Ability

There is no one 'right' or 'wrong' way for any of these: it is all a matter of APPROPRIATENESS. What would go down well in a stockbroker's office might not be effective on a building site—and vice versa.

Practice

Hold some mock interviews based on printed job adverts. Here are some examples. Bring in your own from local and national newspapers.

Jno Croad Ltd.
Small Works Department
require
**Experienced
CARPENTERS**
Telephone R. J. Bowman
for interview
NEWCASTLE 254311

PART-TIME hotel receptionist required approximately 14 hours a week, mainly evenings, pleasant manner and good at figures. — Phone Cobham 382041.

DENTAL RECEPTIONIST, Southsea, to commence October 1. Must have chairside experience. — Write Box No. P307295E, The News Centre, Hilsea, Plymouth PL2 9SX.

Leading Timber & Builders Merchant require a

SALES REPRESENTATIVE

to cover and expand an established territory in this area.
The successful applicant will have a sound product knowledge together with drive and self motivation.
We offer an attractive salary, company car and other benefits normally associated with a large national company.
All applications treated in confidence.
Apply in writing or telephone for an application form to
Mr. G. H. Skinner, Branch Manager

Jewson Ltd.
146, Millbank Street,
Northam,
Bristol,
Telephone 20261

Set up a situation with an interviewing panel (up to five people), a chairperson, and four or five candidates for each job. Interviewees and interviewers can then switch roles.

The interviewees can be themselves or pretend to be somebody else. All the interviewees should have the same qualifications. The one who gets the job will be the one who most impresses by:

—Personality
—Interest
—Attitude
—Honesty
—Alertness

—Friendliness
—Ability to get on with people
—Awareness of the job

Interviewers will be responding to:

—The way you come in
—Handshake
—The way you sit
—Gestures
—Smiles
—Eye movement
—Voice
—Speed, clarity and volume of speech
—Your answers
—Your questions

Questions are likely to be asked on the following subjects:

—Education
—Work experience
—Family
—Reasons for applying
—Future career
—Hobbies/interests
—Health

NB: Both interviewers and interviewees should prepare brief notes on these before the interview. (See pages 32–3 for help with preparation of notes.)

J The prepared talk

For an oral exam, you may need to talk to a group of your friends or to an examiner on a subject in which you are interested. You should speak for at least five minutes and be prepared to answer questions afterwards. Visual aids can be used.

This is an important skill in modern life. In business and industry more explanation is carried out through talks like these than through reading and writing. Being able to talk on a subject that interests you is a useful step in this direction.

Choose the right topic—one on which you can talk confidently and with knowledge. We all speak in a more relaxed way on subjects we know a lot about. Also, try to choose a topic that will interest your audience, though you *can* get them interested in anything as long as your own interest is genuine.

What your talk is about

There are five broad kinds of talk:

1 *Factual*—e.g. Fashion design; How to build a sound system
2 *Narrative* (story)—e.g. A holiday I've enjoyed; A journey I've been on
3 *Descriptive*—e.g. The view from my bedroom; The local park
4 *Humorous*—e.g. The dangers of washing; My relations
5 *Argumentative*—e.g. Ban the bomb?; Capital punishment

● Think of three more talk titles under each heading.

In practice, these divisions often mingle: a narrative will involve some description and some facts. It will certainly benefit from some humour and may well make a serious argumentative point. A humorous talk will probably use anecdote (narrative); and is likely to require humorous description. But it is useful to think in 'types' to get yourself started and to find out where your strengths and weaknesses lie: some of us are less good than others at cracking a joke, telling a story or persuading, for example.

● Prepare one talk from each heading and try it out on a group of fellow students (groups of about 5 are probably best). Let them mark you on each talk and see where they think your strengths lie. Do you agree with their judgements?

● Study the following list. Take each topic in turn and think about *how* you would present it. Would your talk be:

FACTUAL
NARRATIVE
DESCRIPTIVE
HUMOROUS
ARGUMENTATIVE

—or what sort of mixture of these?

Some possible topics for your orals

1 *Corporal/Capital punishment*
  Should the punishment fit the crime? Or do we make society the criminal when we answer murder with murder?

2 *Censorship*
  Should we have the freedom to say and write what we want—or should Big Brother be watching us?

3 *Euthanasia*
  Is there such a thing as killing for mercy—or is it just murder by another name?

4 *Racial discrimination*
  'All blue-eyed people should leave the country.' What do you think?

5 *Generation gap*

6 *Youth unemployment*

7 *Pop culture*

8 *Influence of advertising*

9 *The monarchy*

10 *Apartheid*

11 *Tell the strangest story that ever happened to you*

12 *A foreign country you have visited*

13 *Pets you own*

14 *A travelogue of your home town or village*

15 *A life portrait of someone you admire*

16 *A recent holiday trip*

17 *Your interest in a particular sport*

18 *A club you belong to*

19 *If I could be someone else . . . I would be. . . .*

20 *City versus country life*

Having chosen your topic you need to break it down into sub-headings to think of different aspects.

For example: look at 'The Generation gap' as a topic for a talk. Start by deciding the main point you want to make, e.g., the generation gap is as much the fault of older people as younger people. Then make a list of sub-headings:

1   Things about older people that annoy younger people (rules, attitudes, interests, appearance)

2   Things about younger people that annoy older people (cult groups, attitudes, interests, music, appearance, manners)

3   Light-hearted consequences (dances for different age-groups, situation comedies)

4   Serious consequences (teenage crime, leaving home)

5   Bridging the gap (give and take)

6   Is there really a generation gap or is it generated by the media?

- Break down some of the topics on page 31 in the same way and see which you can get a good range of ideas from. Make some notes on each for a talk.

  If you're stuck, ask questions like
  —How?
  —When?
  —Where?
  —Why?
  —Who?

Some people find it easier to build up ideas by noting them down in the form of a diagram with ideas radiating from the central topic:

A

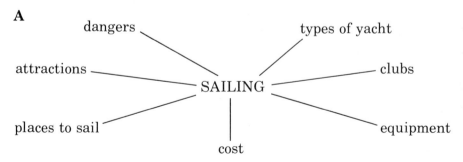

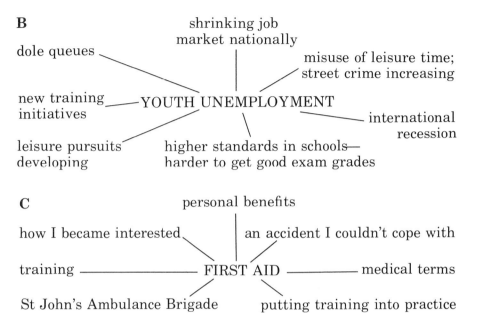

B

shrinking job
market nationally

dole queues

misuse of leisure time;
street crime increasing

new training
initiatives ———— YOUTH UNEMPLOYMENT

international
recession

leisure pursuits
developing

higher standards in schools—
harder to get good exam grades

C

personal benefits

how I became interested

an accident I couldn't cope with

training ——————— FIRST AID ——————— medical terms

St John's Ambulance Brigade

putting training into practice

Practice

1 (*In pairs or individually*)
If you were doing a talk on any of the above, what extra topics would you introduce? Discuss this in a group and draw the diagrams again, with suitable additions.

2 Look at the following list of subjects:

Snooker	My favourite author
Hiking	Musical tastes
Other lifestyles	Motor bikes
Drugs	Nuclear power/war
The video boom	Soccer vandalism
Being a hairdresser	Third World famine
A week's work experience	TV

a) Choose a subject from the above list.
b) Map out points/ideas as in the plans above.
c) Sort them into an order for your talk.
d) Cut out the ones you don't want.

e) Find a powerful starting point and finishing point.
f) Mark with an * where you will introduce visual aids.
g) Mark some areas where you would encourage questions to be asked.

Checklist

Visual aids
Maps
Charts
Slides
Photocopies of pages
Video clip
Photographs
Postcards
Personal project
Collection (e.g., football programmes, rocks, tapes)
Guitar
Computer

NB: Visual aids are to *help*, not to take the place of the talk!

Shape of talk

A good talk has an easily recognizable shape and structure.

1 The topic is introduced.
2 The major points are developed through the main part of the talk.
3 The conclusion is organized and not left to chance.

1 *Introduction*
A strong beginning is needed—often a quote from something somebody else has said works very well. (Look up your topic in a *Dictionary of Quotations* in the Library to see if there is something funny or witty that you can use.)

The introduction should last no more than half a minute during which the audience should be told what the talk is about. It might include some of your own views on the topic in general and the reasons why you chose it.

- Write the outline of an introduction for one of the topics in the list on page 31.

- Choose another topic *not* on the list and write an introduction for it.

2 *Middle*

The beginning and the end of a talk are important because they are often the parts a listener best remembers and they are certainly the parts that create the biggest impression of you as a person. But your important statements, ideas and facts come in the middle section.

What do you need for the middle?

—Plenty of material—enough for at least four minutes.
—3 or 4 important points to make, each of which can be developed.

If, for example, you were talking about drugs, your four main points could be:

a) Difference between various drugs
b) Why drugs are taken – use and abuse
c) Drugs and the law
d) Drugs and young people

—Remember to present ideas in a logical, ordered sequence.
—A visual aid can often remind you of a sequence.
—Diagrams often clarify points you are making. A picture can tell a thousand words.
—Any technical talks (e.g., motor bikes) would demand visual aids. *But* if you are talking about computers, don't just ask the examiner to play with the one you happen to have brought along. Remember it's a *talk* to test your communication skills!

- Write the outline of a middle section for three of the topics listed on page 31.

3 *Conclusion*
—End on a high note.
—Plan your conclusion.
—Don't just say, 'Well, that's it. Any questions?'
—The conclusion should last for half a minute and should attempt to sum up your ideas without just repeating earlier details.

There are many ways of concluding. Which one you use often depends on your subject matter:

a) Draw conclusions from the arguments you have presented. This is often a good way to close material involving strong viewpoints—e.g., nuclear weaponry, vivisection.
b) Use a quotation that neatly ties up what you have been saying. This is effective for a wide range of subjects but is particularly apt where the talk has centred on a point of view rather than on factual material.
c) Refer back to your opening remarks, especially if they were in any way paradoxical, provocative or tongue-in-cheek.
d) Simply finish on your strongest and most powerful piece of evidence, especially if your speech has been of a persuasive nature.

- Write the outline of a conclusion for the two topics you have introductions for, from the topics on page 31.

Checklist

Prepare the talk thoroughly.

Be enthusiastic, especially at the beginning, to gain the audience's immediate attention and hold their interest.

Be warm and friendly.

Look at your audience—share your thoughts with them.

Speak clearly and audibly. Aim at those furthest from you.

Be prepared to answer questions.

And remember:
Gestures
Illustrations
Timing

Use vivid phrases rather than a string of facts, unless the facts and figures are easy to follow and produce a positive effect.

Personal experiences are worth recounting.

Reading

A Why do we read?

We all read for a variety of reasons:

—information from a telephone directory;
—news on a postcard;
—sports results in a newspaper;
—fashion trends in a magazine;
—how much interest in a bank account.

We read for meaning and pleasure.

Most of this is silent/to the self reading.

Reading aloud is a valuable skill which helps your understanding and enjoyment when you read to yourself. When we read aloud, we understand what we are reading more clearly, become more aware of parts we don't understand and are more likely to remember what we have read. There is also an enjoyment in the *sound* of words as well as their meaning. Even when reading silently you should 'hear' it.

You may have to read aloud as part of a spoken English exam and it helps if you can practise doing it.

B Hints for reading

1 *Breathing*
Facing a group or even one person to read aloud to can be daunting and nerve-racking. But, the more you practise, the less nervous you will become. As you get better you will use your nerves to spur you on, just as any good performer does. Actors, musicians, athletes all have to cope with this kind of nervous tension.

It is important to time your breathing so that other people don't notice it. Take several regular deep breaths to relax you at the outset. (NB: A deep breath is *silent*, not a huge gasping sniff!)

2 *Meaning*
Some oral exams allow you to prepare. Others require you to read an unseen passage.

Understand, by reading through to yourself, what the extract is all about. Read to yourself for meaning.

Don't read aloud until you have fully understood it. Some difficult words you may not know the meanings of, but they will usually fall into place in the context of the passage:

- Read the following passage to yourself. Ignore the diagonal lines for the moment.

So Margaret went to the kitchen,(/)and stoked up the fire, and boiled water./// Now, on the tin roof of the kitchen she could hear the thuds and bangs of falling locusts,/or a scratching slither as one skidded down.//Here was the first of them.///From down on the lands(/)came the beating and banging and clanging of a hundred petrol tins and bits of metal.//Stephen impatiently waited while one petrol tin was filled with tea,/hot, sweet, and orange-coloured,/and the other with water.///In the meantime, he told Margaret about how twenty years back he was eaten out, made bankrupt by the locust armies. And then,/still talking,/he hoisted up the petrol cans,(/)one in each hand,/by the wood pieces set corner wise across each,/and jogged off down the road to the thirsty labourers.//By now the locusts were falling like hail on to the roof of the kitchen./It sounded like a heavy storm.//Margaret looked out and saw the air dark with a criss-cross of the insects,/and she set her teeth and ran out into it/– what the men could do, she could.//Overhead the air was thick,/locusts everywhere./The locusts flopping against her,(/)and she brushed them off,/heavy red-brown creatures,(/)looking at her with their beady old-men's eyes(/)while they clung with hard serrated legs./She held her breath with disgust and ran through into the house./There it was even more like being in a heavy storm./The iron roof was reverberating, and the clamour of iron from the lands was like thunder.

Doris Lessing: *The Habit of Loving*

Even if you don't understand 'serrated', 'reverberating', 'clamour', you can probably understand the gist of the passage. If it's a prepared reading you'd look them up and check the pronunciation—you'd be expected to. But if it's an unseen, the examiner is not going to attach too much importance to individual words. Just say them confidently, without stumbling—and don't worry about them. It's your reading of the whole passage that counts, not your ability to say a few 'hard' words.

Work out where you will pause—always at full stops. New paragraphs demand a longer pause.

Try not to run out of breath mid-sentence. You won't if you've taken in the whole sentence. But if it's a *long* sentence it's better to break it down into sensible phrases than to be choking for lack of breath. The important thing is to know *when* to breathe.

In the above passage some possible breathing spaces have been marked.

/ = pause briefly; 'snatch' breath (quietly, don't gasp!)
// = longer pause
/// = major pause; big breath (still quietly)
(/) = quick breath if you have to

• Try reading the passage through aloud a few times until you can control the breathing spaces naturally—you may well change some of them after a few experiments.

3 *Mood/atmosphere*
What is the mood of the passage? Violent or humorous? Full of suspense or fear?

How will you convey the mood? Will you try to read a little more quickly for exciting bits, or a little more loudly for violent bits?

• How would you describe the moods of these passages? Read them through to yourself.

a) When Mr Bilbo Baggins of Bag End announced that he would shortly be celebrating his eleventy-first birthday with a party of special magnificence, there was much talk and excitement in Hobbiton.

b) That night they heard no noises. But either in his dreams or out of them, he could not tell which, Frodo heard a sweet singing running in his mind: a song that seemed to come like a pale light behind a grey rain-curtain and growing stronger to turn the veil all to glass and silver, until at last it was rolled back, and a far green country opened before him under a swift sunrise.

c) Over the lip of the little dell, on the side away from the hill, they felt, rather than saw, a shadow rise, one shadow or more than one. They strained their eyes, and the shadows seemed to grow. Soon there could be no doubt: three or four tall black figures were standing there on the slope, looking down on them. Frodo thought that he heard a faint hiss as of venomous breath and felt a thin piercing chill. Then the shapes slowly advanced.

(J. R. Tolkien: *Lord of the Rings*)

d) I lived with a man once who used to make me mad that way. He would loll on the sofa and watch me doing things by the hour together, following me round the room with his eyes, wherever I went. He said it did him real good to look on at me, messing about. He said it made him feel that life was not an idle dream to be gaped and yawned through, but a noble task, full of duty and stern work. He said he often wondered now how he could have gone on before he met me, never having anybody to look at while they worked.

(Jerome K. Jerome: *Three Men in a Boat*)

- Now read the passages aloud, conveying their mood. The pitch of your voice helps here:

  —Lower pitch for dark and mysterious subjects. Usually quiet and not too fast—be careful not to become inaudible. (Try passage c.)

  —Higher pitch for bright, witty and cheerful passages. Usually brighter, louder and quicker—but be careful not to gabble. (Try passages a and d.)

  Most important—try to *put yourself into* the setting of the passage: then you will automatically convey the mood to your audience.

Practice

With a partner or in a group, try saying each of these phrases in as many different ways as possible to convey different moods, feelings, meanings. Discuss what you think each change of tone suggests:

—'I'm sorry.'
—'No.'
—'What's the matter?'
—'Not now.'
—'Please stop.'
—'What did you say?'

4 *Speed*
- Read the following poem aloud as fast as you can, but still clearly. Your partner can stop you every time he/she doesn't 'catch' a word. Keep practising till you can really get it fast and clear.

To sit in solemn silence in a dull, dark dock,
In a pestilential prison with a life-long lock,
Awaiting the sensation of a short sharp shock,
From a cheap and chippy chopper on a big black block.

(W. S. Gilbert: The Mikado)

(The operas of W. S. Gilbert and Arthur Sullivan are full of passages like these, called 'patter' songs. If you enjoyed this one, or need more practice, try the songs that begin:

'When you're lying awake with a dreadful headache' (From *Iolanthe*)
'I am the very model of a modern major General' (From *The Pirates of Penzance*)
'As some day it may happen that a victim may be found' (From *The Mikado*)
'Oh! A private buffoon is a light-hearted loon' (From *The Yeomen of the Guard*)

But when you read aloud to a group for the first time, or under nervous pressure, you will probably go at least twice as fast as you should.

- See how *slowly* you can read this passage:

  So on they went, slowly, slowly, inch by inch, feeling their way amidst the narrow crevices, as they climbed painfully down to the dark, dank, depths of the seemingly bottomless pit. No plants grew here. No creatures grazed. All was black, baleful, lonely as an endless night, longing for the morning that would never come.

Most passages, of course, are neither as fast as the first nor as slow as the second, but in between and involving moments of both extremes.

You must take sufficient time to:
—pronounce all words clearly.
—pause after important statements.
—let your listener take in the sense.

You can tell the 'speed' of a passage by its mood—but most passages don't need to be gabbled or dragged. They need *variety* of pace—some bits faster, some slower.

- Read the following passage to yourself, ignoring the underlining marks.

It was nearly October and the day had seen the passing of full rain clouds across the sky. As I walked over the grass of the park and under the trees, the big clouds were crowding together and it looked like rain. Lines of beech trees on the rising ground stood out like bones against the dark. Up and down the small hills and down again, so that I imagined it was the ribbed skeleton of a long and ancient animal lying there. The grass and heather of the park were worn out from the summer and they felt old and fragile under my shoes as I went. It was not a good day and I seemed to be alone there. No people, no animals and hardly a bird. It was quiet and still and waiting for the rain.

The rain came in round, marble drops, rattling in the trees, drumming among the grass and causing the heather to tremble. The clouds seemed to be climbing on each other's backs in their hurry and the splashes joined together into a downpour. Now, I thought was the time to go back, really. I was under a tree and none of the rain was coming on me, but now was the time to make up my mind whether to go on or not. If I returned my steps now—or anyway after the rain had stopped—there was a good chance that I would not have been missed, and I would have dodged Matron's Bible Class, which was always a good thing.

(Leslie Thomas: *This Time Next Week*)

In this passage, a suggested pattern of speeds has been marked for you.

················· = faster than normal

− − − − − − − = slower than normal

────────── = very slow

Notice how the words of the passage guide you to the speed: 'dark', 'lying there', 'old', 'worn out', 'quiet', 'still', 'waiting'—they're all slow words. 'Climbing on each other's backs in their hurry' wants to be read much faster.

- Now read the passage aloud, following the suggested speed markings. You'll probably have to try it more than once. Then try varying the speed your *own* way.

- Mark up and read the following passage, paying particular attention to variations of speed:

The clock indicated eighteen minutes to nine.

The players took up their cards, but could not keep their eyes off the clock. Certainly, however secure they felt, minutes had never seemed so long to them!

'Seventeen minutes to nine,' said Thomas Flannagan, as he cut the cards which Ralph handed to him.

Then there was a moment of silence. The great saloon was perfectly quiet; but the murmurs of the crowd outside were heard, with now and then a shrill cry. The pendulum beat the seconds, which each player eagerly counted, as he listened, with mathematical regularity.

'Sixteen minutes to nine!' said John Sullivan, in a voice which betrayed his emotion.

One minute more, and the wager would be won. Andrew Stuart and his partners suspended their game. They left their cards, and counted the seconds.

At the fortieth second, nothing. At the fiftieth, still nothing.

At the fifty-fifth, a loud cry was heard in the street, followed by applause, hurrahs and some fierce growls.

The players rose from their seats.

At the fifty-seventh second the door of the saloon opened; and the pendulum had not beat the sixtieth second when Phileas Fogg appeared, followed by an excited crowd who had forced their way through the club doors, and in a calm voice, said, 'Here I am, gentlemen!'

(Jules Verne: *Around the World in Eighty Days*)

- Choose some passages of your own and 'mark them up' in this way. Experiment with different speed effects and see which work best.

5 *Rhythm*

The pattern of words in a sentence also requires stress and rhythm when you read aloud. This comes from the mood and the meaning of a sentence. The punctuation also gives a good guide to rhythm as the writer intended it.

- Read the extract above again, deciding which words need special emphasis or stress.

- Now read the following sentences. Where does stress have to be placed? Where and why is rhythm important? Discuss and read in groups. Let each person have a go at reading the sentence in a different way. Which ones work?

a) Night after night, week after week, month upon month, the neighbours were disturbed by the dead girl's spirit.

b) Disgusted, I tore it off the hook, its throat ripped open, and threw it out into the middle of the stream where it sank rapidly.

c) They saw it but for a glimpse, for the window was instantly thrust down; but that glimpse had been sufficient, and they turned and left the court without a word.

d) Tomorrow, and tomorrow, and tomorrow,
   Creeps in this petty pace from day to day,
   To the last syllable of recorded time;
   And all our yesterdays have lighted fools
   The way to dusty death.

   (Macbeth)

6 *Words to enjoy*
   Writers enjoy words. So should readers!

   In b) above did you read 'ripped' in a juicy blood-red way or did you just say it as if it was an ordinary word like 'was'?

   In c) did you enjoy the sound of 'thrust' or did you just treat it like 'put'?

   In d) nearly every word is worth enjoying—like a tasty meal!— 'creeps', 'petty pace', 'recorded time', 'lighted fools', 'dusty death' all have something special in their sound to be enjoyed. Make sure your hearer can enjoy them too.

   Look in your passages for words and phrases that sound particularly good and let your audience hear not only the sense of the writing but the pleasure it can give.

   Look especially for ALLITERATION (words containing the same sounds) e.g., petty pace, dusty death, solemn silence, prancing pony—it's easy to spot and can always be used expressively. Don't waste it.

● Look through any of the passages in this section. What examples of alliteration can you find?

   The following passage is an extract from a radio talk. It depends for its effectiveness on picking out the words that can be 'enjoyed' and finding ways of making them fun for the reader and her/his listeners:

   The personal wonders that have brightened my life are many and varied, and high on the list—and how happy I am to be able at last to give it a public word of thanks—is my hot water bottle. No possession that has come my way on Life's Highroad has ever given me greater satisfaction. It hasn't, of course, always been the same hot water bottle. Hot water bottles come and go, or rather, they come and leak and go. I'm breaking in a new one at the moment—delicately ribbed and in a rather striking shade of pink, and already a real pal. It warms up my pyjamas before I climb into them, and then it gets busy warming outlying portions of me. And there's another advantage. Waking in the night, I just stick out a toe and the bottle's heat, or reduced heat, tells me just where we are—2.40, 4.15, or 6.50, with dawn over the horizon. Some people enshroud their bottles in covers. Not me. I like them naked and unashamed and giving off their full rich and rubbery aroma.

(Arthur Marshall)

7 *Individual words*
Always open your mouth and move your lips/tongue precisely when reading aloud. Sound each word distinctly. Don't slur words one into the next.

• Think up twenty pairs of words with the same beginnings but different endings. Then say them to your partner. He/she must put them into a sentence to show that they understand which word you are saying. See how often they think you're saying a different word from the one you think you're saying. Here are some to start you off:

| socks | sing | death | field | feel | prism | fairy | limp |
| socks | sink | deaf | filled | fill | prison | ferry | lip |

(sobs)

8 *Volume*
If you are speaking or reading aloud to an examiner sitting opposite you, there should not be any problems, though the tendency here can be to mutter shyly.

In a larger room, you should read to the back row though try to take in the whole room with your eye movements. Speaking loud enough does not mean you have to shout. You may need to shout to convey anger in a passage but listeners should not feel bombarded by your voice.

• Practise reading aloud the passages on pages 38–45. Ask a partner to listen and to comment on your use of volume.

9 *Accents*
A regional accent is in no sense 'bad English'. A Welsh, Cockney, or West Indian accent does not matter: 'audibility, clarity, liveliness and interest' are what the examiners are looking for and the same will be true in other situations.

Be natural. If the opportunity arises to imitate other accents in the passage (e.g. in dialogue), have a go. It's fun and brings the characters to life.

- Read the passage *Willy* (page 53), to your partner, using different accents for the speakers. Then listen to him/her reading it. Discuss the best way of reading what the characters say.

Checklist

General hints for the oral examination

Don't worry about outside noises. The examiner is on your side.

Don't rustle pages nervously.

Don't shuffle from foot to foot or turn away from your audience.

Don't worry about a slip of the tongue. It's not a test of nerves. If it's important, correct it clearly and firmly (just as news-readers do). Otherwise just carry on.

Remember:

WHAT YOU DO RIGHT IS MORE IMPORTANT THAN WHAT YOU DO WRONG.

Do hold your book or paper up, but don't let it cover your face—and your voice.

Do sit or stand straight and look the examiner in the eye. It gives a good confident start and helps your voice.

Do look up from the text at suitable points. This keeps your listener's interest. If it's a prepared reading, you can mark in the places where you'd do this.

And remember:

—Read the passage through carefully to yourself first.
—Speak clearly.
—Be confident—the examiner wants you to pass.
—Tell yourself that you are *very* good, just as you go in.

C Reading passages

The following passage has been marked in a way to suggest the kinds of thing you should think about when you're preparing a reading.

- Try to read this passage in the ways indicated. First read it to yourself; then read it aloud.

Cheese

(a) I remember a friend of mine buying a couple of cheeses at Liverpool.(b) //
(c) Splendid cheeses they were,(d)/ripe and mellow,(e)/and(f) with a two-hundred horse-power scent about them that might have been warranted to carry three miles(/)and knock a man over at two hundred yards.(g)//I was in Liverpool at the time and my friend said that(/)if I didn't mind(/)he would get me to take them back with me to London/as he would not be coming up for a day or two himself(h)/and he did not think the cheeses ought to be kept much longer.//

'Oh, with pleasure, dear boy,' I replied,(i)/'with pleasure.'///

I called for the cheeses and took them away in a cab./It was a ramshackle(j) affair, dragged along by a knock-kneed,(k) broken-winded somnambulist,(l) which his owner,(m)/in a moment of enthusiasm,(n)/referred(o) to as a horse.(p)//I put the cheeses on the top and we started off at a shamble that would have done credit to the swiftest steam-roller ever built,(q)/and(r) all went merry as a funeral bell until we turned a corner.(s)//There,(t)/the wind carried a whiff from the cheeses full on our steed.(u) It woke him up,(v)/and,(w)/with a snort of terror, he dashed off(x)/at(y) three(z) miles an hour.///

(Jerome K. Jerome: *Three Men in a Boat*)

Key points

(a) Start with the voice moderately loud. This is not a passage that calls for much variation in volume. It should sound fairly conversational.

(b) 'Cheeses' is the important word in this sentence. Enjoy it!

(c) (d) (e) Slow down to emphasize and enjoy these descriptive words.

(f) Then speed up to emphasize the humour—it will sound best if you can go from here to the full stop in one breath.

(g) Allow time for the humour of the preceding phrase to sink in and also to give yourself a good breath and get your voice up to volume, in case it's dropped.

(h) Slow down a little here to emphasize the important stages in the development of the story. The audience has got to feel that these things are significant, though they don't yet know why.

(i) Highlight the anticipation of the story. Perhaps a wicked smile is needed with the repeat of the words 'with pleasure', which should be slower than the first time.

(j) (k) (l) Emphasize these colourful descriptive words. Enjoy the slow, heavy quality.

(m) (o) Notice how important the commas are here in bringing out the full sarcasm of this comment.

(n) Emphasize the sarcasm.

(p) A strong sarcastic emphasis—almost a snort—is needed on 'horse'.

(q) Very emphatic—we need to expect something fast!

(r) Very scornful—even a swift steam-roller is very slow.

(s) This can go faster as if really happy. This will emphasize the sarcasm.

(t) Another word to enjoy—for reader and audience. Let the voice rise on it.

(u) 'Our steed' is a very grand phrase for this broken-down old horse. Use rather a pompous tone.

(v) Use the commas to emphasize the dramatic quality here and create suspense.

(w) 'Snort' is a word to enjoy—give it a snorting emphasis.

(x) This part is quite fast, but still bring out the vigour of 'dashed'.

(y) A nice pause here can highlight the anti-climax of 'at three miles an hour'. Be careful that the voice is rising on 'off' so that it doesn't sound like the end of the sentence.

(z) Slow and emphatic to bring out the plodding gait of the horse.

/ = short breath
// = longer breath
/// = pause
(/) = snatch a breath if you need to

- Notice how much there is to think about even in a short passage like this. In the same way now work out how to read several passages of your own choice. Mark them as you would a piece of music with indications of soft, loud, faster, slower, pauses, emphases, where the voice would go up and down etc. You could work out a colour code for each of these things, e.g., blue for pause, red for emphasis, yellow for slow, green for soft.

- Here is another passage from *Three Men in a Boat*. Mark it out for reading and practise reading it aloud.

And then we got on to drains, and that put George in mind of a very funny thing that happened to his father once. He said his father was travelling with another fellow through Wales, and, one night, they stopped at a little inn, where there were some other fellows, and they joined the other fellows, and spent the evening with them.

They had a very jolly evening, and sat up late, and, by the time they came to go to bed, they (this was when George's father was a very young man) were slightly jolly, too. They (George's father and George's father's friend) were to sleep in the same room, but in different beds. They took the candle, and went up. The candle lurched up against the wall when they got into the room, and went out, and they had to undress and grope into bed in the dark. This they did; but instead of getting into separate beds, as they thought they were doing, they both climbed into the same one without knowing it—one getting in with his head at the top, and the other crawling in from the opposite side of the compass, and lying with his feet on the pillow.

There was silence for a moment, and then George's father said:

'Joe!'

'What's the matter, Tom?' replied Joe's voice from the other end of the bed.

'Why, there's a man in my bed,' said George's father, 'here's his feet on my pillow.'

'Well, it's an extraordinary thing, Tom,' answered the other; 'but I'm blest if there isn't a man in my bed, too.'

'What are you going to do?' asked George's father.

'Well, I'm going to chuck him out,' replied Joe.

'So am I,' said George's father, valiantly.

There was a brief struggle, followed by two heavy bumps on the floor, and then a rather doleful voice said:

'I say, Tom!'

'Yes!'

'How have you got on?'

'Well, to tell you the truth, my man's chucked *me* out.'
'So's mine! I say, I don't think much of this inn, do you?'

(Jerome K. Jerome: Three Men in a Boat)

- Listen to some records/tapes of good professional readers and make notes of how they use their voices. (See page 85.)

Checklist

Choosing your own passage:
1 Choose a passage you really like.
2 Look for passages with some speech in—these make for lively reading.
3 Choose passages with strong descriptive words.
4 Humorous or adventurous passages are often most successful, especially if some kind of suspense is involved.

And remember:
—Volume
—Tone
—Pitch
—Rhythm
—Pace
—Stress
—Pause
—Atmosphere
—Enjoyable words

One of the most enjoyable ways of improving your reading aloud is through the reading of plays. The more experience of this you can get, the better. Making a tape can be fun and gives you the chance to hear whether your reading is as clear and lively as you thought. Even reading a play on to tape by yourself (or with one friend) taking *all* the parts, can teach you a lot about keeping it interesting and making your voice flexible.

- Most valuable of all is verse reading. Even the simplest poem depends on how you say it. How many different ways can you find to say this?

I must go down to the sea again,
To the lonely sea and the sky.
I've left my shoes and socks there,
I wonder if they're dry.

(Spike Milligan)

- Now try something more complex. Think of all we've said about pitch, pace, stress, rhythm, volume, tone, mood, atmosphere and enjoying words. Prepare a reading of the following poem. You won't get it 'right' first go, but the more often you try the more you'll find in it and the more enjoyable it becomes:

Then before breakfast down toward the sea
I ran alone, monarch of miles of sand,
Its shining stretches satin-smooth and vein'd.
I felt beneath bare feet the lugworm casts
And walked, where only gulls and oyster-catchers
Had stepped before me to the water's edge.
The morning tide flowed in to welcome me,
The fan-shaped scallop shells, the backs of crabs,
The bits of driftwood worn to reptile shapes,
The heaps of bladder-wrack the tide had left,
(Which, lifted up, sent sandhoppers to leap
In hundreds round me) answered 'Welcome back!'
Along the links and under cold Bray Hill
Fresh water pattered from an iris marsh
And drowned the golf-balls on its stealthy way
Over the slates in which the elvers hid,
And spread across the beach. I used to stand,
A speculative water engineer—
Here I would plan a dam and there a sluice
And thus divert the stream, creating lakes,
A chain of locks descending to the sea.
Inland I saw, above the tamarisks,
From various villas morning breakfast smoke
Which warned me then of mine; so up the lane
I wandered home contented, full of plans,
Pulling a length of pink convolvulus
Whose blossoms, almost as I picked them, died.

(John Betjeman: 'Summoned by Bells')

Reading—a final note

With reading—as with talking, listening and writing—practice can make perfect. But after working at your reading over and over again, in the ways shown here, the best thing you can do for the exam itself is *read naturally*.

Just as learning to walk took a lot of effort, a lot of practice and a lot of falling over, so learning to read well takes repeated trial and error. But in the end you don't have to think about *how* you're going to walk: similarly, the best readings are spontaneous, fresh and natural. But you will only achieve this if you work hard now.

D Answering questions orally on a reading passage

Look again at the reading passage entitled *Cheese* (page 47). Here are the kinds of question you could be asked. Notice that some test your *understanding*. But some are asking for your *response* (your ideas, reactions, feelings).

Some are closed questions with simple answers, but the more interesting ones are open questions allowing you to develop your answer more fully.

- Answer the following questions:

    a) What made the horse move faster than normal?
       (Closed question to test understanding.)
    b) Do you think the cheeses sound very tasty?
       (Open question requiring explanation of answer—not just yes or no. Needs your opinion.)
    c) What do you think makes this a funny story?
       (Open question. Needs to show understanding and response.)

Some suggested answers are given on pages 88–9. Compare them with your own and discuss the differences and similarities.

Now read the following passage:

Willy

Willy went to the yard door and put his eye to the crack by the hinges. He couldn't see anything and a whistling draught made him blink. There were feet playing hopscotch outside, somebody was kicking a tin can, somebody else was bouncing a ball. The sun and the smell of the warm, rainwashed air went to Willy's head. He drew the bolt of the door, opened it, and peered out.

The hopscotch stopped at once. 'Look who's here!' yelled one of the players, a big boy of eight with a thatch of red hair. 'Little Willy Overs who's too good to play with us. Ooh, don't he look sweet, don't he just, in his little woolly stockings and his nice clean boots!'

'Bet yer old man don't know you're here!' screeched another. 'Bet he'd give you a leathering if he cotched you. Him and his old ginger whiskers!'

Willy looked warily behind him. Certainly he did not want his mother to hear any of this. He knew quite well that he was not allowed to unbolt the door.

'He's looking for his mammy,' jeered the redhead. 'Mammy's little pet in his little woolly stockings. Shall we blow his nose for him?'

'I'm going for a walk,' said Willy in a trembling voice.

'He's going for a walk!' parroted two or three voices with contemptuous disbelief.

'With his little reins to stop him falling down!' added the redhead. He was two years older than Willy and sometimes came into the shop to buy sweets. He was very different then in front of Mr Overs and within reach of The Stick.

'I'm going to the Park,' said Willy, and with legs shaking with fear, he marched down the cobbles. There were hoots and yells behind him, but nobody followed, and he got to the end of the passage, where it came out in Crown Street.

He just could not go back again, straight into the mob of boys. The only other way was down Audley Street and in at the shop door. But his father and The Stick were there. At the thought of The Stick his legs went faster and he ran down Crown Street, to the start of his first Great Adventure.

(Avery: *A Likely Lad*)

- Write down answers to these questions.
1 What does Willy do that is against his mum's rules?
2 Why do you think she's set down a rule like this?
3 Do you think it was a good idea to keep Willy in like this?
4 What sort of things do the other children laugh at him for?
5 Who do you think The Stick might be?

Try to use answers to questions on the passage to establish a friendly conversational tone. Don't treat it like a stiff, formal exam! Even here, your personality should come across.

 Now check your answers with the suggested answers on pages 89–90.

E Questions on set books

In a way these are easier to answer than those on a passage you have not seen before and you can spend more time preparing them, knowing that you're killing two birds with one stone as this work may come into your literature written examination too.

Here are a few of the kinds of questions you could be asked on *any* book. Adapt them to your book and try them out on a friend.

Checklist 1

> a) Is your book more interesting for its story, its characters or its ideas?
> b) Which part of the book do you like best? Why?
> c) Which character do you like best? Why?
> d) Do any of the characters change during the book? Give an example. What makes him/her change?
> e) Where does the book take place?
> f) What are the main ideas behind the book and what do you think the writer is trying to say about them?
> g) Did you consider this a well written book? Why?/Why not?

Listening

A Memory/recall

However hard you listen, you won't gain much unless you remember what you're told. How often have you asked someone the way and forgotten it even before they've finished telling you?

Here are some exercises to help build up memory.

1 **Memory test** (*Whole class or small groups*)
Take about twenty items. Place them on a tray. The contestant(s) concentrate hard for a minute and then the tray is taken away. The contestant then has to name as many of the items as he/she can remember in a minute. If twenty's too easy, increase the number. If it's too hard, try fifteen.

2 **Sound detectives** (*Whole class*)
Close your eyes and listen for the nearest sound you can hear, the farthest away, the loudest, the softest, the highest and the lowest.

The class keep their eyes closed. The leader (a student or the teacher) walks quietly around the room and makes a series of sounds (about five to start with). Open eyes and try to identify the sounds in order. As the class get more experienced, the number of sounds can be increased and they can be made more unusual and harder to identify.

3 **Build a sentence** (*Pairs or small groups*)
Each person takes it in turns to add to a sentence. Each time the whole sentence must be said and each time it must be a *complete* sentence. You're out when you can't remember, get it wrong or can't add any more. For example:

A: She went to the pictures.
B: She went to the pictures on Saturday.
C: She went to the pictures on Saturday afternoon.
A: She went to the pictures on Saturday afternoon but couldn't get in.
B: She went to the pictures on Saturday afternoon but couldn't get in because of young children.

C: She went to the pictures on Saturday afternoon but couldn't get in because of young children who had been waiting for over an hour.

You get better with practice. Here are some more starters:

1   She wore a red tie.
2   She bought an ice-cream.
3   He ran along the road.

4   They were sitting in the park.
5   They went to the beach.
6   Her dad was late home.

B Listening to a reading

But even being able to repeat like a parrot doesn't show you've understood (though it does show you've listened). We listen in order to receive communication. Note that there are different kinds of communication we listen to—narrative, descriptive, argumentative, factual. Each of these calls on different listening skills.

1   Narrative

Narrative is easiest—we are following a story: even young children find a story easy to remember. But keep an ear open for the significance of the story (its meaning), and the way certain words and phrases bring this out.

• Try the following in pairs.

Decide who is **A** and who is **B**.

A plays the 'teacher' role, **B** the student. **B** can close his/her book now.

A (to **B**): 'After I've read the passage you've got to tell me what happened and what you think the writer's point was—why he bothered to write the story.'

A then reads out the following:

The Wind and the Sun

The North Wind and the Sun were having an argument as to which was the stronger, and they agreed to try their strength on a traveller. The one that got the traveller's cloak off first was to be the winner.

The North Wind began, and blew a strong, cold blast, accompanied by a sharp, driving shower of rain. But instead of blowing the man's cloak off it only made him hold it round his body more closely.

The Sun's turn came next and he began to shine as hotly as possible upon the head of the poor weather-beaten traveller. The man grew faint with the heat, and, unable to bear it any longer, he threw off his heavy cloak and took shelter in a neighbouring wood.

 Answer on page 90.

• Now swap over and let **B** do the reading and questioning and **A** be the listener and answerer.

Belling the Cat

Some mice lived in a house where there was a fierce cat.

Even in the dark night they could not stir from their holes without being pounced upon, and it was difficult for them to get anything to eat. One day they all met together to find a way of escape.

'I'll tell you what to do,' said a young mouse. 'It's quite easy. Tie a bell round the cat's neck. As the cat walks the bell will ring, and we'll know where he is.'

At this speech the mice squeaked for joy, until an old mouse asked:

'But who will bell the cat?'

None of them dared!

 Answer on page 90.

• **A** does the reading again and **B** keeps his/her book closed. Careful listening is needed here to work out exactly what has happened:

His eyes scrutinized the great curtain of the mountains with a keener inquiry.

For example, if one went so, up that gully and to that chimney there, then one might come out high among those stunted pines that ran round in a sort of shelf and rose still higher and higher as it passed above the gorge. And then? That talus might be managed. Thence perhaps a climb might be found to take him up to the precipice that came below the snow; and if that chimney failed, then another farther to the east might serve his purpose better. And then? Then one would be out upon the amber-lit snow there, and half-way up to the crest of those beautiful desolations.

He glanced back at the village, then turned right round and regarded it steadfastly.

He thought of Medina-saroté, and she had become small and remote.

He turned again towards the mountain wall, down which the day had come to him. Then very circumspectly he began to climb.

When sunset came he was no longer climbing, but he was far and high. He had been higher, but he was still very high. His clothes were torn, his limbs were blood-stained, he was bruised in many places, but he lay as if he were at his ease, and there was a smile on his face.

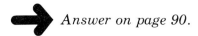 *Answer on page 90.*

This passage is a very good one for reading practice, as it depends very much on getting the pauses right and giving the significant parts sufficient emphasis.

2 Description

In listening to description we rarely expect to retain all the details. What we need is an overall impression.

- Discuss the overall impression produced by each of these passages. Again work in pairs and alternate reader and listener:

a) Stradhoughton Moor was a kind of pastoral slum on the edge of the town. It was fringed on Moorside by the dye-works, Stradhoughton Town football ground, and some public lavatories. The centre of the Moor was paved with cinders, where generations had tipped their slag and ashes, and where the annual fairs were held. There was a circumference of sparse yellow grass where the old men walked in summer, and I took the path they had worn towards a pocket of stone cottages, mostly condemned, that huddled miserably together in a corner of the Moor. Behind the cottages Stradhoughton Moor rose steeply again, out of an ashpit, to meet the scraggy allotments and, beyond them, the real moors of Houghtondale, such as were illustrated in the Council yearbook.

(Keith Waterhouse: *Billy Liar*)

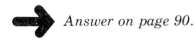 *Answer on page 90.*

b) The bright Monday morning ring of the clocking-in machine made a jarring note, different from the tune that played inside Arthur. It was dead on half-past-seven. Once in the shop he allowed himself to be swallowed by its diverse noises, walked along lanes of capstan lathes and millers, drills and polishers and hand-presses, worked by a multiplicity of belts and pulleys turning and twisting and slapping on heavy well-oiled wheels overhead, dependent for power on a motor stooping at the far end of the hall like the black shining bulk of a stranded whale. Machines with their own small motors started with a jerk and a whine under the shadows of their operators, increasing a noise that made the brain reel and ache because the weekend had been too tranquil by contrast, a weekend that had terminated for Arthur in fishing for trout in the cool shade of a willow-sleeved canal near the Balloon Houses, miles away from the city. Motor-trolleys moved up and down the main gangways carrying boxes of work—pedals, hubs, nuts and bolts—from one part of the shop to another.

(Alan Sillitoe: *Saturday Night and Sunday Morning*)

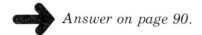 *Answer on page 90.*

c) It was a queer little isolated place, in a dell surrounded by old pine woods that were black and forbidding at night. A humped shoulder of down cut it off from the sunset, and a gaunt well with a shattered penthouse dwarfed the dwelling. The little house was creeperless, several windows were broken, and the cart-shed had a black shadow at midday. It was a mile and a half from the end house of the village, and its loneliness was very doubtfully relieved by an ambiguous family of echoes.

(H. G. Wells: *The Food of the Gods*)

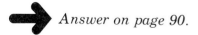 *Answer on page 90.*

d) The South Coast, even so, was not what I'd been led to expect—from reading Hardy and Jeffery Farnol—for already it had begun to develop that shabby shoreline suburbia which was part of the whimsical rot of the Thirties. Here were the sea-shanty-towns, sprawled like a rubbishy tidemark, the scattered litter of land and ocean—miles of sea-shacks and bungalows, apparently built out of wreckage, and called 'Spindrift' or 'Sprite o' the Waves'.

(Laurie Lee: *As I Walked Out One Midsummer Morning*)

(What impression of the South Coast did the writer have before he visited it? What sort of thing did he actually find? What was his attitude towards it?)

3 Argument

For most people the most difficult listening is following an argument. Yet it is also the most important listening—think of Parliament, the law courts, business meetings, even school: they all depend on being able to follow and understand other people's ideas. Just as with narrative we listen for a story, so with argument, we listen for the points being made.

The most important thing is to grasp the *main* idea. Once you've identified this, the details follow more easily. *Usually*, speakers or writers move from the general (the main idea) to the particular (the details) so the main idea *often* comes first. But beware of exceptions and of clever speakers who deliberately mislead you as to their real subject by starting on an apparently irrelevant course.

- Try these in pairs. **A** to read. **B** to close book and jot down notes, then *say* what he/she thinks the passage is about in general (the main idea) and in particular. Alternate the roles of reader and note-taker.

 Suggested answers are on page 91. Compare them with your own answers.

a) Watching coal-miners at work, you realize momentarily what different universes people inhabit. Down there where coal is dug it is a sort of world apart which one can quite easily go through life without ever hearing about. Probably a majority of people would even prefer not to hear about it. Yet it is the absolutely necessary counterpart of our world above. Practically everything we do, from eating an ice to crossing the Atlantic, and from baking a loaf to writing a novel, involves the use of coal, directly or indirectly. For all the arts of peace coal is needed; if war breaks out it is needed all the more. In time of revolution the miner must go on working or the revolution must stop, for revolution as much as reaction needs coal. Whatever may be happening on the surface, the hacking and shovelling have got to continue without a pause, or at any rate without pausing for more than a few weeks at the most. In order that Hitler may march the goosestep, that the Pope may denounce Bolshevism, that the cricket crowds may assemble at Lord's, that the poets may scratch one another's backs, coal has got to be forthcoming. But on the whole we are not aware of it; we all know that we 'must have coal', but we seldom or never remember what coal-getting involves. Here am I, sitting writing in front of my comfortable coal fire. It is April but I still need a fire. Once a fortnight the coal cart drives up to the door and men in leather jerkins carry the coal indoors in stout sacks smelling of tar and shoot it clanking into the coal-hole under the stairs. It is only very rarely, when I make a definite mental effort, that I connect this coal with that far-off labour in the mines. It is just 'coal'—something that I have got to have; black stuff that arrives mysteriously from nowhere in particular, like manna except that you have to pay for it. You could quite easily drive a car right across the north of England and never once remember that hundreds of feet below the road you are on the miners are hacking at the coal. Yet in a sense it is the miners who are driving your car forward. Their lamp-lit world down there is as necessary to the day-light world above as the root is to the flower.

(George Orwell: *The Road to Wigan Pier*)

b) A good driver has many things in his make-up. Some of these, such as experience and skill, will come only in time. But others—just as important—must be part of him from the start. These qualities are a sense of responsibility for the safety of others, a determination to concentrate on the job of driving, patience and courtesy. Together, these become what is generally known as a driver's attitude.

Not everyone is patient by nature or gifted with good powers of concentration. But because attitude is so important a part of safe driving, every driver must make a real effort to develop these qualities—and this effort must start from the very beginning of his first driving lesson.

Getting into the right attitude will be harder for some people than others. It can be more difficult than the actual business of learning to make the car go or stop. All the things which go to make up attitude are just as necessary for the experienced driver as for the learner.

(Department of Transport: *Driving*)

c) Parents' evenings are not only educationally unsound, but also a complete and utter waste of time. I speak from bitter experience, for over the years as both teacher and parent, I must have attended more than a hundred of these unprofitable get-togethers. It is my heart-felt opinion that they have very little value, educational or otherwise.

Problems start when a note is 'sent out' to parents inviting them to attend school or college to discuss their offspring's progress. This note is foolishly given to the pupil, who may or may not take it home. Often it will lie crumpled at the bottom of a satchel, discovered only after parents have made other (unbreakable) arrangements for the evening in question.

In some cases the failure to deliver may be deliberate. One student recently confided to me that she *never* presented such an invitation to her parents. That would be 'asking for trouble'.

As a parent I am always pressed into attendance at such events for my children seem anxious that I should make public my interest in their progress.

In my alternative role I know only too well that the parents of those children with serious learning difficulties rarely come to a parents' evening. So teachers don't see those who really need their counsel. Perhaps it would be better if teaching staff called on these parents at home, to discuss problems more informally.

Of course, many parents do attend these functions, which usually results in long queues forming in front of teachers, who are lined up behind desks ready for the onslaught. Appointments made in advance are invariably missed or overrun, and tea and biscuits do little to appease those waiting. Most infuriating is the man just in front of you who says 'I'll only be five minutes', and then spends half an hour expounding on his daughter's mathematical genius.

I'm convinced that parents always know beforehand what they are going to hear. Of course, it may be 'edited' a little, for teachers cannot be entirely truthful for fear of upsetting people too much. After three hours of fruitless double-talk, both teachers and parents go home tired and irritable. If son or daughter is waiting up anxiously for the verdict, the scene is set for a blazing row. Future efforts are not likely to be improved and the child may go to school next day with a real grudge against the teacher.

Let's face it, none of us likes to be talked about when self-defence is impossible, so why should our children? Let's do away with parents' evenings once and for all and rely on more accurate methods of assessment, such as written reports and examinations, which give a truer picture of children's abilities—and save a lot of frustration into the bargain.

(Alison Edwards: *She*)

C Listening tests

Now that you've worked on some of the skills that go towards effective listening, it's time to try a passage of the kind you might get in an exam. Remember that this kind of listening skill is also needed for board meetings, committees, the organization of clubs and societies and simple everyday situations: none of us can get by without a high level of listening skill.

- Read the following examination passage and look at the sorts of note that have been made alongside the text. These are the kinds of thing that might go on in your head as you *hear* the passage read to you the first time through. All you're really trying to do is follow what the passage is about. The words underlined are the ones that guide you through the main ideas. Listen out for them!

The first sentence is always very important

You won't find a single hair dryer in the Wig Department of the Royal Opera House, Covent Garden. There are rollers and pins galore, gallons of shampoo, lacquer and conditioner, combs and brushes of every kind. 'But when it comes to setting and drying hair, we bulk dry in a special oven,' explained wig master Ronald Freeman.

Try to remember special names for things or people

Every wig used in a Covent Garden opera or ballet production is made by Ron and his assistants. It can take up to five days to make a wig, depending on the style. Strands of hair are carefully knotted into the *lot of time and work* base—a skill which demands concentration, as well as a steady hand. Knotting can become extremely tedious so, when they want a change, the wig-makers *Try to see this in your mind* weave the hair on to strings of cotton. 'This is used for making very long wigs. We sew each one to make a ladder effect,' said Ron. 'The longest one so far was two metres!'

The hair comes, ready dyed, from a hair merchant. *hair bought* European hair has a silkier texture than Asian hair and is much more expensive. 'Although we use some artificial hair, you can't compare it with the real thing.' *another 'special term'*

One of the tools they use is a hackle, which looks like a hand-sized bed of nails. It is used to comb a mixture *see it!* *streaks* of colours through a bundle of hair. The different shades create a more natural effect under stage lights.

The department make receding hair lines and bald patches by painting layers of plastic on to a head form. When it's dry, the plastic peels off and is then styled to fit the wearer.

Ron and his assistants also make everything from false noses and plastic masks to beards, moustaches and eyebrows. And just once in a while, a designer will ask them for—would you believe—a hairy chest.

(Welsh Joint Education Committee, 1981)

After that there is usually a second reading of the passage during which you should listen out for the *details*. Some examination boards let you see the questions *before* the second reading (which is easier, though the questions and passages tend to be harder); others do not let you see the questions until after you have finished hearing the passages (which is a more severe test of memory). Check with your teacher what is going to happen with *your* examination board.

- Here are the questions that were asked on the above passage.

1 How are the wigs of the Royal Opera House set and dried?
2 Name two qualities required by anyone knotting strands of hair into the base of a wig.
3 Explain the differences described in the passage between European and Asian hair.
4 How is the hackle, which is used for combing colours into the hair, described in the passage?

5   As well as wigs, Ronald Freeman and his department make other items. Name three of them.

These would be easy enough as comprehension questions—the difficulty lies in *remembering*. Hence the importance of the memory exercises on pages 55 and 56. Keep practising these.

• Now apply the same techniques to this test which can be done in pairs or small groups or as a whole class.

Person **A** reads the passage (it needs to be a good reading, so it must be thoroughly prepared) and follows the timing instructions. Person **B** (or everybody else) does the test.

Everyone except **A** should now *close the book*.

The passage to be read is on pages 91–3.

Read it aloud clearly, but at normal pace. The **B** students must not take any notes during this reading.

After the first reading, tell them to turn to the questions below.

1   a) How old was Lydia when she came to Britain?   (*1 mark*)
    b) What is her husband's occupation?   (*1 mark*)

2   Give TWO reasons why her father decided that he and his family should leave Czechoslovakia.   (*2 marks*)

3   Although Lydia was brought up in Czechoslovakia she and her mother had Hungarian passports. Why was this?   (*1 mark*)

4   What proved to be the advantage of possessing Hungarian passports rather than Czech ones?   (*2 marks*)

5   Give THREE facts we learn about Mrs Kemeny's personality and character.   (*3 marks*)

6   Explain fully how Lydia came to speak English fluently.
                                                            (*4 marks*)

7   Give TWO reasons why Lydia thinks she was able to settle happily and quickly in Britain.   (*3 marks*)

8   State ONE of the two ways in which her Czech childhood influences her life as an artist.   (*1 mark*)

9 How does Lydia think that her mixed background has influenced her personality? (*4 marks*)

Total: 22 marks

- Now re-read the passage. Tell the **B** students that this time they may make notes.

  After the second reading, tell the **B** students that they have 3 minutes to finish their notes. They may not start writing their actual answers. Finally they have twenty minutes to complete the answers as they would in the examination. (In practice, you can stop when the last one has finished).

- Now discuss your answers and the difficulties you encountered, hear each other's answers and decide on the best ones. This should be done in groups of six or less.

 Suggested answers are on page 93. But don't look at these until you've discussed your own in some detail. Your answers may well be better than the ones suggested!

- Of course in real life (and some exams) you don't hear everything twice. So now have a go at the following listening test which allows you one reading only—and you don't see the questions until you've heard the passage.

  All students should now *close their books* except the one who is to read the passage and conduct the test (Student **A**).

  Student **A**— read this out to the other students:

  'This passage is set in Manchester at the beginning of the century. Willy is twelve years old, and will soon be leaving elementary school unless he is able to go on to grammar school. He has won a scholarship, but his father refuses to let him go, because he wants Willy to start work.

  Whilst I am reading you are allowed to make notes, but you may not use shorthand. The reading will last for about eight minutes.'

  The reading is on pages 94–6.

Now tell the other students to open their books and answer the questions below. They must *not* look at the reading passage. They are allowed twenty minutes.

1   What are Willy's feelings as he runs away from home? (*4 marks*)

2   You are told in the introduction that Willy is only twelve. What other evidence is there that Willy:
a) looked young;
b) behaved childishly?   (*4 marks*)

3   How do the appearance and manner of the mill hand who stands up for Willy win Willy over and persuade him to give up the tandem?   (*5 marks*)

4   What makes Willy begin to be suspicious of the two youths?   (*2 marks*)

5   What brings Willy to his full senses?   (*1 mark*)

6   What reasons could Willy have for wanting to think it was all a joke?   (*3 marks*)

 Discuss your answers and compare them with the suggested answers on page 96.

Checklist 2

While the passage is read, listen very carefully. If your mind starts to wander, focus on listening for the full stops. That way you *have* to follow the sense.

Don't over-concentrate on little details you may not understand. Get the overall meaning first.

Read questions carefully. Don't rush.

Take notes if the situation (or exam board) allows you to.

D Listening situations

Listening in an examination is only a *test* of your ability to listen in life. The more you practise these skills, the better your preparation for the exam will be—and the better your competence in the exam tests, the more prepared you'll be for listening effectively in real-life situations.

1 *Interviews* (see pages 22–9)
Remember that the ability to listen to your interviewer intelligently is as important as your confidence in speaking.

2 *Radio/TV programmes*
We're listening all the time—unless we just use them as meaningless background. Telling a friend about 'last night's telly' is good oral work. Seeing if you can follow a radio talk is even better.

3 *Telephone messages*
A very useful and realistic demonstration of the importance of listening. Unfortunately, it is virtually impossible to practise these in the classroom, though they can be built into drama work. Take advantage of any real opportunities to use the telephone, including answering at home and taking messages for the family.

Combining the skills

A Talking and listening and reading

- You will need a chairperson. Elect one from your group; take it in turns to chair the group.

  We now want a panel of 'experts'. You will have to do some background work, collecting information together from newspapers, magazines, TV news, and so on.

  Choose from the following subjects:

1 The recent rise in crime
  Roles: citizen, policeman/woman, criminal, politician, community spokesperson

2 Should Britain be a nuclear power?
  Roles: Anti-nuclear demonstrator, pacifist, politician, army representative

3 Effect of television on the family
  Roles: Teenager, parent, TV programme-maker, social worker

4 Vandalism in large towns
  Roles: Shopkeeper, football fan, policeman/woman, publican, local resident, football manager

  You, the expert, will have to make a short statement in the early part of the discussion, so jot down your information in a logical order (see pages 32–6). Have some information left over, for the questions which will follow your statement.

  When you have had a discussion in a small group, open up the discussion to the whole group.

B Role plays

In the following three role play exercises all notes on characters are given to the whole group. Read these carefully, then decide in your groups who will play which parts. Act out the scenes, remembering all that you have learned about talking and listening skills.

1 Court-martial

Lieutenant Stephen Mark, His Majesty's Navy, second-in-command of the destroyer, HMS *Victorious* in 1945, slowly comes to the conclusion that his Captain, John Barnett, is mentally unstable and, in a moment of emergency at the height of a fierce sea storm, invokes special naval regulations and relieves him of his command in order to save the ship from sinking. This is a very serious action which leads automatically to Mark's court-martial for mutiny.

- Act out the trial. What is your group's final verdict?

Cast
Officers of the Court

Rear-Admiral Trench, Presiding Officer
Two Officers of the Court

The Prosecution Counsel

Lieutenant-Commander Sitwell

The Prosecution Witnesses

Captain John Barnett
Captain Edward Summers (Medical Officer)
Mrs John Barnett
Commander William Blake (navigational expert)
Able-Seaman Wynn Jones (Orderly to the accused)

The Defence Counsel

Lieutenant-Commander Hughes

The Defence Witnesses

Lieutenant Stephen Mark
Captain Samuel Wilks (Psychiatric Officer)
Mrs Dora Bucknall
Captain Hans Scroeder
Able-Seaman Clive Green

The Prosecution Witnesses

Captain John Barnett
Aged 45. Captain of HMS *Victorious* (destroyer) and formerly Captain of minesweeper HMS *Valiant*. Married 18 years. Distinguished naval record, being decorated for bravery and outstanding battle achievements five times. Responsible for sinking six German U-boats.

His crew know him as a strict, uncompromising and often bad-tempered Captain, often moody and quarrelsome after drinking but in action brave and daring. Many of his successes were achieved (in the crew's opinion) through apparently reckless and foolhardy behaviour. Called by his crew 'Old Iron Guts'.

Claims that on the night in question (16 May 1945) there was a heavy and fierce sea-storm. At about 21.00 hours the navigator detected underwater movement on the radar which the Captain stated to be a U-boat and ordered battle stations. Captain Barnett ordered the change of course into the storm in order to avoid being in the sights of the submarine's torpedoes and in doing so was challenged by Lt. Mark who claimed the underwater movement was in all certainty not a submarine and that turning into the storm meant certain disaster.

Captain Barnett, furious at this insubordination, ordered the Lieutenant to his quarters whereupon Lt. Mark stated that the Captain was not in full control of his mental faculties and according to Articles 195 and 196 of the Naval Code took command of the ship and altered course out of the storm.

Captain Edward Summers
Aged 59. Medical Officer of HMS *Victorious* and formerly of the minesweeper HMS *Valiant*. Served under Captain Barnett on four ships in the last twelve years. Great personal friend of the Captain's. In his quarters on the night in question. Heard the alarm for battle stations and started to prepare the medical room for casualties. Called by Petty-Officer Anderson to administer a sedative to the Captain at about 21.30 hours. Found the Captain in a fury in his cabin having been locked there by the Second-in-Command, Lt. Mark, who, he was informed, had taken command of the ship. After speaking to the Captain, Summers went straight to Lt. Mark and asked by what authority he had taken charge of the ship. Was told

Captain was deranged. Summers stated that his objection to this 'mutiny' was to be put on record. In his opinion the Captain was in full command of his faculties and though often subject to violent fits of temper and to moodiness, was as sane as the next man and quite capable on the night in question of holding command of the ship.

Mrs John Barnett
Wife of Captain John Barnett. Married 18 years. Her husband is a generous and trusting man and although at times bad-tempered and moody, was at all times normal and well-adjusted. Never been treated for mental illness though once had some nervous trouble.

Commander William Blake
Navigational expert. Called to give specialist evidence. Not on the destroyer at the time. In his opinion Captain Barnett acted quite correctly in changing course to avoid the submarine's sights. If the ship had continued on the same course it would undoubtedly have been an easy target for torpedo. However, in altering course into a fierce sea-storm he was taking a great risk of turning the ship over. If there was not a submarine below the HMS *Victorious* the Captain acted very foolishly to turn the ship and the action would not have been one of a rational man.

Able-Seaman Wynn Jones
Aged 26. Orderly to the accused, Lt. Mark. Found Captain Barnett, though firm and often bad-tempered, just and courageous and admired him. Found Lt. Mark conceited and full of his own importance and ambitious to become a Captain. Many times Jones heard him in conversation with other officers saying how the Captain was an incompetent and a madman and how he could command the ship better than him if he were blindfolded. Always complaining about the Captain and saying how he was treated like an irresponsible schoolboy.

The Defence Witnesses

Lieutenant Stephen Mark
Aged 34. Second-in-Comand of HMS *Victorious* (destroyer). Unmarried. Highly commendable Naval record, achieving highest honours for seamanship and navigational studies at Dartmouth. Awarded the Distinguished Naval Cross for gallantry in 1941 and mentioned in Despatches for bravery.

The crew know him as a shrewd, self-willed and often arrogant officer who on several occasions questioned the Captain's orders. Known to have quarrelled with the Captain on several occasions. Fellow officers know him as a most ambitious sailor, very enthusiastic, thorough and brave. Not a particularly likeable person and intolerant of mistakes. Claims that on the night in question Captain ordered a complete change of course into a fierce and menacing sea-storm in order, in the Captain's words, to avoid sailing in the sights of a U-boat that was supposedly directly beneath them. Checking the radar scanners and seeing what could not have possibly been a submarine, Lt. Mark questioned the Captain's order and accused him of endangering the crew's lives by deliberately sailing into a typhoon. At this point, Lt. Mark claims the Captain ordered him from the bridge and fell into a furious and uncontrollable rage, shouting abuse at him and calling him a coward. Lt. Mark, seeing clearly that the Captain was unbalanced, took command of the ship, locked the Captain in his cabin and steered the ship out of the storm. Checking the scanners immediately after this action, he found there to be no sign of Captain Barnett's supposed U-boat.

Captain Samuel Wilks
Psychiatric Officer. Called to give specialist evidence. Not on the ship at the time. Disagrees with Captain Summers (Medical Officer). When questioning Captain Barnett prior to the trial, found him to be a man of violent temper and nervous disposition with a tendency to paranoia (persecution mania). In his opinion the Captain was not a brave and courageous man but just a foolhardy and foolish one and had probably won all his medals for mad exploits which would never have been attempted by any normal man. On the night in question Dr Wilks states that what probably happened was that Captain Barnett had a fit of temper and steered the ship directly into a storm to avoid an imaginary submarine. He (Captain Barnett) showed under hypnotism to have a deep-seated obsession for destroying submarines and this partly explains his odd behaviour on the night in question and his actions with regard to Captain Hans Scroeder.

Mrs Dora Bucknall
Widow of the late Major Thomas Bucknall, Royal Engineers. States that several weeks before this incident took place Captain Barnett

and his wife attended a cocktail party at her home in Portsmouth. Her husband (who was then alive—he has since been killed in action) had cause to ask Captain Barnett to leave the party after an incident where he insulted another guest and started to shout and cause a disturbance. In her opinion he had been drinking heavily and seemed incapable of controlling his fierce temper. When her husband asked him to leave, Captain Barnett's fury increased and he struck her husband several times, causing him actual bodily harm. In her opinion Captain Barnett is a madman and ought to be locked up.

Captain Hans Scroeder
Commander of the German U-boat 34, destroyed in action by Captain Barnett while in command of the minesweeper HMS *Valiant* in 1942. Captured after the sinking of his submarine. After being picked up in his life raft, Scroeder was taken to the Captain's cabin where he was questioned. When he refused to give more than his rank, Barnett flew into a mad rage, struck him across the face and threatened that he would get all the information he wanted or Scroeder would be keelhauled. Scroeder was then locked up in a small dark cabin in the hold of the ship and not given food or water for several days. When he was finally allowed out, Captain Barnett clubbed him with a bottle in an attempt to extract information. Scroeder was in a coma for three days. Barnett had told the Medical Officer and crew that Scroeder had attacked him and he had defended himself. In the opinion of Scroeder, Captain Barnett was a sadistic and deranged man who had fits of uncontrollable temper. (The Prosecution point out Scroeder is a POW and naturally hates Barnett for sinking his submarine and ridiculing him in front of his men.)

Able-Seaman Clive Green
Aged 24. Radar operator. In his opinion the object on the scanner was not a submarine though he could have been mistaken. In fact on two previous occasions he had doubted the Captain's opinion, only to be proved wrong. Disliked the Captain's manner and way of treating the crew and had been given harsh treatment when called before the Captain for a minor offence in which Lt. Mark took his part.

2 A Case of Murder

On 1 December, 1970 Lord Claud Icebottom (Baron Brinsworth) and his wife held a party at their home, Icebottom Hall. During the party Lady Icebottom collapses. Examined by Sir Cornelius Crab (a guest at the party), she is found to be dead. A post-mortem reveals she died as the result of a large quantity of arsenic. Chief Inspector Ivor Truncheon investigates.

- Act out the trial. What is your group's final verdict?

Cast

The Accused

Major Fergus Ffarquenharsen-Ffortescue, MC

The Defence

The Rev. Donald DoGood
Alderman Arbuthnot Ardlugs, Mayor of Brinsworth
Mrs Ardlugs, Mayoress of Brinsworth
Bertram Bayleaf, Chief Gardener at Icebottom Hall
Tadger McBadger, Turf Accountant
Dermot O'Dung, Manager of fertilizer factory
Penelope Pinchme, maid at Icebottom Hall
Charles Marbles, butler at Icebottom Hall

Crown Witnesses

Chief Inspector Ivor Truncheon
Dr Doris Berryham, MB, police pathologist

The Prosecution

Lord Claud Icebottom, Baron Brinsworth
Sir Cornelius Crab, FRCS, MD
Lady Cassandra Crab
Percy Potion, chemist
Mrs Poppy Potion
Donna Headshrinker, psychiatrist
Eustacia Clutterbuck

Major Fergus Ffarquenharsen-Ffortescue, MC
The accused. Aged 50. Major in Royal Greenjackets. Born 1920.

Educated Ponsonbury Preparatory School, Eton College. Joined army in 1937. Trained at Sandhurst until 1942 when gazetted as lieutenant. Became Captain in 1955, Major in 1965. Explosives expert. Has knowledge of poisons. Spent 1968–70 in Northern Ireland where he commanded a Bomb Disposal Unit. Responsible for defusing dangerous splinter bomb in Belfast in 1969. Decorated MC. Bomb exploded in his face causing serious facial disfigurement, the loss of sight in one eye and possible brain damage. Sent to Catcliffe Military Hospital for intensive medical aid and recuperation. On extended leave. While at this hospital met Lady Greta Icebottom who was visiting the wards in her capacity as Patron. Invited to soirée on 1 December.

Prosecution forward as motive: Major was former fiancé of Lady Icebottom (née Greta Gargoyle). After a fierce argument (due to the defendant's vicious temper and inordinate jealousy) the engagement was broken off.

Prosecution argue the defendant is suffering from acute brain damage caused by the bomb explosion in April, viz. paranoia (mental derangement characterized by delusions and hallucinations) and, possessed of a fanatical jealousy, he premeditated the death of the woman he once loved but then despised for marrying another. He went to the party, the Prosecution claim, with the clear intention of murdering her.

Prosecution try to establish:
1 The major's unbalanced mind
2 His knowledge of lethal poison
3 His paramount motive
4 His opportunity

It is claimed he arrived at the party at 8 p.m. and, after heated argument with his victim on the terrace, slipped a lethal dose of arsenic into her champagne.

The Defence

The Rev. Donald DoGood
Visited Catcliffe Military Hospital in his capacity as Vicar where he met the defendant. Found him 'a delightful man, full of fun and energy, a charitable, likeable, good-natured sort'. In his opinion (as a scholar of human nature) the defendant could never kill anyone

cold-bloodedly. Considers it 'churlish' that a man who has served his country so well should be rewarded with this barbaric treatment.

Alderman Arbuthnot Ardlugs
Councillor, Alderman and Mayor of Brinsworth (1969–70). Married with three children—Irma, Ethel and Ernest. Arrived at cocktail party at about 8 p.m. with his wife. Met the defendant in the hallway and found him a charming and very informative person. Learnt about his heroic exploits in Northern Ireland, about his MC and the injuries he received. Remembers the major left him about 9 p.m. (clock chimed) to talk to the hostess. They retired to the terrace. In his opinion the major remained calm, relaxed and good-humoured all evening in contrast to Lord Claud who was nervous, fidgety and constantly watching his wife.

Mrs Amanda Ardlugs
Supports her husband's testimony. She found the major 'quite nice'.

Bertram Bayleaf
Gardener at Icebottom Hall. Employed there for the last four years. Dislikes his job since 'the gaffa' (Lord Claud) gives him far too much work and far too little money. Has vast estate gardens to keep in order with their large lawns, numerous hedges and flower beds. Gives evidence that Lord Claud is a loud-mouthed, quarrelsome, miserly individual who was always shouting at his wife who was always 'on the bottle'. On evening in question was trimming privet hedge near terrace when at about 9 p.m. (heard church clock) saw Lady Icebottom come on to the terrace accompanied by the defendant. Far from arguing, the gardener states 'they were on very friendly terms, very friendly indeed'.

Tadger McBadger
Turf Accountant. Not at the party. Owns three betting shops. Lord Claud owed him over £400 after heavy losses on the horses. Promised to pay him soon as he was 'coming into a lot of money'. States that it is common knowledge that Lord Icebottom depended on his wife for money and that they never got on.

Dermot O'Dung
Manager of a fertilizer factory. Supplies Lord Icebottom with manure and fertilizer. A close friend of Lady Greta before her death. Finds Lord Claud a 'bad-tempered, conceited, crashing bore' who constantly provoked his long-suffering wife into arguments. On

evening in question states he arrived at the party for 8 p.m. Spent half an hour talking to Percy Potion before being introduced to the mayor and the defendant. The latter he found pleasant and sociable, the former rather worse for drink. Refers to local gossip that Lord Claud is an inveterate gambler and 'womanizer' and that he was only waiting for his wife's death to inherit her considerable fortune.

Penelope Pinchme
Maid at Icebottom Hall. Gives evidence that Lord Claud was a spendthrift, 'full-of-his-own importance' and on one occasion he grabbed her on the stairs. Disliked him and states his wife was an alcoholic whose 'breakfast was a bottle of gin'. On the evening of the murder was serving drinks when (at about 9 p.m.) she saw Lady Greta collapse. She then screamed and fainted.

Charles Marbles
Butler at Icebottom Hall. Found 'the master' quite intolerable— demanding, bad-tempered, forever shouting and complaining. Such a contrast to his last master Lord Flunkett Plunkett, Viscount Vichwater whom he served for 20 years. Given the arrangements for the wedding anniversary dinner. Serving drinks on the evening of the murder. Remembers announcing the guests, one of whom (Major Ffortescue) he found polite, well-spoken and likeable. During the course of the evening Lady Greta collapsed. Lord Claud then phoned for the police and ambulance.

Crown Witnesses

Chief-Inspector Ivor Truncheon
Arrived at the scene of the crime at exactly 9.32 p.m. accompanied by Sergeant Everard Bootbrain and Policewoman Gladys Gaskett. Made a list of all the guests present and proceeded to take statements from each. The defendant he found relaxed and at ease, Lord Claud irate and demanding the arrest of the major whom he accused of the murder 'of his dear wife'. After making certain enquiries into the backgrounds of the guests, arrested the major and charged him with the murder. The major stated on being cautioned 'You must be mad, I'd never murder her, I couldn't. He's to blame, that wastrel she married, he did it.'

Doctor Doris Berryham, MB
Police pathologist. Examined the body. Cause of death—death by poisoning. A large quantity of arsenic was found lining the stomach

wall. Time of death—around 8–9 p.m. Other ingredients found in the stomach reveal it was most certainly rat poison that was used.

The Prosecution

Lord Claud Icebottom
Aged 60. Husband of the murdered woman. 14th Baron Brinsworth. Came into title on the death of his father in 1940. Married ten years later to Lady Greta Gargoyle, daughter of Sir Gunther Gargoyle. No children. Manages large estates in Catcliffe, Canklow and Brinsworth. States that on the evening in question (1 Dec.) invited a number of friends to a celebration party for his wedding anniversary. Remembers his wife in high spirits but accounted it due to an excess of alcohol. His wife 'had a predilection for drink'. About 7 p.m., before the party commenced, he recalls having a slight difference of opinion with his wife ('no more than a tiff') over the invitation of Major Ffortescue whom he knew to be 'an old flame'. States that at 9 p.m. his wife collapsed in agony, clutching her stomach. Examined by Sir Cornelius Crab, she was found to be dead. He immediately phoned the police and ambulance.

Defence put forward certain evidence:
1 Lord Icebottom in 1950 was impoverished and it is suggested he married Lady Greta for her money. She was known to have a large personal fortune of over £600,000.
2 Gossip in the locality is that Lady Greta is more in love with her title than with the man. She was interested in her status as a peeress.
3 He was heavily in debt with Tadger McBadger, the turf accountant.
4 The butler and maid give evidence concerning the unhappy state of the marriage.

Sir Cornelius Crab
Famous Harley Street surgeon and close friend of the Baron whom he has known for 25 years. Knows him as a man of integrity, intelligence and acumen. Arrived at the party at about 8.30 with his wife. Talked with his host until about 9 p.m. when he saw Lady Greta collapse on the floor. Examining her he found her to be dead. He suspected poison but said nothing so as not to cause alarm. He and his wife overheard a heated conversation between Lady Icebottom and the defendant as they walked past the terrace. The

snippets they heard included 'If you don't come away with me I'll make you sorry you ever met me'; 'I'll make you rue the day you married that pompous clown!'.

Lady Carmelina Crab (Cassandra)
Supports everything her husband says.

Percy Potion
Aged 40, married with three children—Paula, Penny and Peasmold. Owns four chemist shops. Secretary of the local Conservative Association of which Lord Claud is the President. Always found Lord and Lady Icebottom 'a charming, well-matched, happy couple'. On night of murder arrived at the party at about 8 p.m. with his wife Poppy and chatted for about ten or fifteen minutes with Mr McDung about the load of fertilizer he had recently delivered. About nine o'clock Lady Greta fell to the floor in agony and was attended by a guest.

The Prosecution ask this witness to relate how the defendant bought a quantity of poison from his shop for 'killing a particularly vicious rat'.

The Defence establish that Lord Claud also purchased some arsenic for disposing of moles which burrowed under his lawn.

Mrs Poppy Potion
Wife of the above, supports her husband's testimony and adds that Lady Greta had confided in her that very evening that she was afraid of somebody at the party. When she said this, states Mrs Potion, 'she looked directly at the defendant, Major Ffortescue'.

Miss Donna Headshrinker
Consultant psychiatrist at Catcliffe Military Hospital. The defendant is under her care and receiving treatment for the condition paranoia where the patient is subject to irrational fears and beliefs and hallucination. Gives evidence that he may very well have felt rejected and depressed on meeting the woman he once loved, and determined to kill her. Under hypnosis he is revealed to be a hard, ruthless man, very courageous and determined.

The Defence refer to the defendant's medical record which shows he was making quite remarkable steps in his recovery and to the fact that the psychiatrist is only guessing—her evidence is not fact.

Miss Eustacia Clutterbuck
Close friend of Lady Greta. Aged 50. Unmarried. Arrived at the party at 8.10 p.m. to find it 'in full swing'. States she left the party before the tragedy at about 8.45 p.m. States that she remembers the defendant when he was engaged to Lady Greta and his nature: bad-tempered, jealous, demanding, cold. Met him at the party and found 'he hadn't changed one bit'. Gives evidence that the marriage of Lord and Lady Icebottom was 'on the rocks'. She loathed him and him her. It was only a matter of time before they got a divorce. Asked if she thought Lord Claud capable of murdering his wife she states 'he's too weak and cowardly. All he's bothered about is gambling and spending Greta's money'.

Points to note

The Defence attempt to discredit the evidence of the Prosecution witnesses. Defence aim to present Lord Claud Icebottom as a hard, ruthless, calculating scoundrel who cruelly provokes his wife into fierce quarrels, who married her merely to get his greedy hands on her money, who chases after other women and who gambles like a madman. The motive and opportunity are stressed.

The Prosecution attempt to discredit the Defence witnesses' testimonies. Prosecution aim to present Lord Claud as a noble peer of the realm, a grief-striken widower whose wife collapses and dies a horrible death before him. The defendant is presented as a madman, a psychopath whose mind was deranged by the explosion and who carefully planned the brutal murder of the woman who threw him over for another.

3   Cowboy Trial

Mat Wooster, ranch-hand on the 'Lazy B' ranch, Tombstone, is accused of robbing the Tombstone bank and killing the manager on 2 May 1864. Arrested by the Sheriff two days later he was found to possess 400 dollars in mixed, used bills, 40 dollars in gold coin, a carbine rifle, and a box of 404 cartridges.
Wooster pleads 'Not Guilty'.

- Act out the trial. What is your group's verdict?

Cast

The Court

Circuit Judge Jeffrey

The Accused

Mat Wooster

The Prosecution

The Counsel for the Prosecution
The Prosecution Witnesses:
   Mrs Perkins, widow of the bank manager
   William Webb, bank clerk
   Mrs Allot, storekeeper
   Mrs Elisha Eliot, client of the bank
   'Red' Bates, ranch-hand

The Defence

The Counsel for the Defence
The Defence Witnesses:
   Major Berkeley, owner of the 'Lazy B'
   'Rory' Calder, ranch-hand
   'Rio Rita', Saloon 'gal'
   Joe, barman at 'The Silver Dollar' Saloon

The Court Witnesses

The Sheriff
The Doctor

Mat Wooster
The Accused. Aged 36. Ranch-hand on the 'Lazy B' ranch. Accused of robbing the Tombstone bank and killing the manager, and stealing 400 dollars in mixed used bills and 40 dollars in gold coin. Fellow ranch-hands know him to be a loud-mouthed, often bad-tempered, moody and argumentative cowboy subject to fits of depression caused largely through lack of money. Has reputation of being an excellent shot but prefers to use a carbine rifle rather than a colt. Wooster claims that on the afternoon of the robbery (2 May) he was branding cattle and rounding up steers with 'Rory' Calder in

the north pasture of the 'Lazy B' ranch. He was engaged in this business from dinner time until about 3.30 p.m. when he returned with Calder to the ranch.

The Prosecution

Mrs Perkins
Widow of the murdered bank manager. Remembers her husband telling her of a visit from Wooster several weeks before the robbery and asking her husband for a loan of 200 dollars to start a ranch. Having no securities the manager refused Wooster a loan, whereupon Wooster raged furiously, banged on the desk and threatened the manager, calling him 'a tight-fisted, purse-pinching old miser'.

William Webb
Remembers the occasion that Mrs Perkins speaks of when Wooster came for the loan. He conducted Wooster into the manager's office and after a moment heard Wooster shouting words to the effect: 'You tight-fisted old miser'.
Served at the bank on 2 May and witnessed robbery.
Robber the same build as Wooster, wore a red checked shirt, fancy waistcoat, high boots with spurs, a brown neckerchief around the face. Remembers distinctly the ears of the robber: long, with hairy lobes, exactly the same as the accused. Robber caried carbine rifle. Ordering everyone against the wall of the bank, the robber asked him (the clerk) to fill an old saddle-bag. The manager went for a gun which was under the counter but was shot by the bandit. The robber ran with the saddle-bag full of money. He (the clerk) then ran for the Sheriff.

Mrs Allot
Storekeeper. Was sweeping the front of the store on the afternoon in question. The store is across from the bank. She gives evidence that she heard a shot in the bank and a few minutes later saw a masked figure run out, carrying a gun and a saddle-bag. The man was dressed in a blue cotton shirt, fancy leather waistcoat, high boots with spurs and had a brown silk scarf wrapped around his neck. He leapt on his horse and rode off. She then informed the Sheriff.

Mrs Elisha Eliot
Client of the bank. Was present in the bank when it was robbed. Transacting business at the counter when a masked man burst in and ordered her and the rest of the people there to face the wall at

the far end of the bank. She heard him demand the money in the till and heard the shot. The criminal had a brown silk scarf round his face and wore a blue checked shirt and a waistcoat. She remembers the spurs jingling as the outlaw walked over to the counter, the rifle and the cold steely blue eyes.

'Red' Bates
Ranch-hand at the 'Lazy B' ranch. Had fight with Wooster after he made fun of him. Tells the Court how Wooster wanted to start his own ranch but was always complaining about not having any money. Remembers the occasion when Wooster came back to the ranch having been refused a loan from the bank and remembers Wooster calling the manager 'miser' and how 'he'd get his own back'.

The Defence

Major Berkeley
Owner of the 'Lazy B' ranch. Hired Wooster eight months before the robbery. Always found him a most reliable, hard-working and intelligent worker though a little quick-tempered and moody. Wooster had approached him for a loan but the Major had refused because Wooster could provide no securities. Wooster had accepted this without bad feeling and said he would get the money from the bank.

On the day in question the Major had sent 'Rory' Calder and Wooster up to the north pasture to finish off the cattle branding and steer rounding. Saw both men set off at about 12 o'clock. The north pasture being a good eight miles from town, it would be (almost) impossible for Wooster to have got into town, robbed the bank and returned to the ranch. He remembers what Wooster wore on that day: suede jerkin, brown ankle boots and (he thinks) a brown shirt and neckerchief.

'Rory' Calder
Works on the 'Lazy B'. Accompanied Wooster up to the north pasture on the day in question and remained there all afternoon returning to the ranch about 3.30 p.m.

'Rio Rita'
Saloon help. Remembers Wooster coming into the saloon a day after the robbery and being very generous, spending a great deal of money. Remembers his being in a card game with the gambler

James Buchanan. They both left the saloon about 9 p.m. to continue the game in Buchanan's room. Wooster returned to the saloon about an hour later and had a great deal of money on him. Wooster claimed he had won all the money in a gambling game. Buchanan has since left town.

Joe
Barman at the saloon. Substantiates Rita's story. Wooster was in gambling game with Buchanan but seemed to be losing in the early part of the evening. Both men left about 9 to continue the game in a hotel room. Wooster returned and spent over 50 dollars at the bar. He noticed a wad of notes in Wooster's coat as he paid for the drink.

Court Witnesses

The Sheriff
Proceeded to the 'Lazy B' two days after the robbery, acting on the evidence of the bank clerk and Mrs Perkins who claimed they recognized the accused as the outlaw. On searching the accused's bunk found 400 dollars in notes and 40 dollars in gold coin. Also took possession of a carbine rifle and 40 rounds of 404 cartridges. The prisoner professed his innocence but came quietly. The sheriff noted that the rifle had been fired quite recently (within the last few days).

The doctor
Examined the body of the manager and found a 404 cartridge embedded in the heart. The man died immediately, having been shot at short range by a carbine rifle of the type owned by the accused.

Resources

A Readings on records and tapes

The comprehensive 'Spoken Word Catalogue' published by **Gramophone** (177 Kenton Road, Kenton, Harrow; Tel: 01-907 4476) is well worth looking at—there are almost certainly recordings of all your set books for literature examinations as well as recordings that should give pleasure to a wide range of listeners of all ages and backgrounds. Here is a selection of fifteen:

Jane Austen: *Emma* Read by Prunella Scales
　ARGO SAY 27 (double cassette)
Arthur Conan Doyle: *Four Sherlock Holmes Stories* Read by Robert Hardy
　ARGO SAY 2 (double cassette)

Robert Graves: *I, Claudius* Read by Derek Jacobi
ARGO SAY 16 (double cassette)
Richmal Crompton: *William Stories* Read by Kenneth Williams
ARGO SAY 4 (double cassette)
Richard Adams: *Watership Down* Read by Roy Dotrice
ARGO ZSW 574-7 (discs); K30K 44 (cassettes)
J. R. R. Tolkien: *The Hobbit* Read by Nicol Williamson
MCOR 105-7 (cassettes)
Richard Burton—a Personal Anthology
ARGO ZDSW 714 (disc); KZDSC 714 (cassette)
Henry Williamson; *Tarka the Otter* Read by David Attenborough
LISTEN FOR PLEASURE TCLfP 7034 (double cassette)
John Wyndham: *The Day of the Triffids* Read by Robert Powell
LISTEN FOR PLEASURE TCLfP 7097 (double cassette)
George Orwell: *1984* Read by Derek Jacobi
LISTEN FOR PLEASURE TCLfP 71405 (double cassette)
Gavin Maxwell: *Ring of Bright Water* Read by Christopher Timothy
LISTEN FOR PLEASURE TCLfP 7075 (double cassette)
Alistair MacLean: *Where Eagles Dare* Read by Martin Jarvis
LISTEN FOR PLEASURE TCLfP 7084 (double cassette)
Graham Greene: *The Third Man* Read by James Mason
LISTEN FOR PLEASURE TCLfP 7103 (double cassette)
John le Carré: *Smiley's People* Read by the author
LISTEN FOR PLEASURE TCLfP 7106 (double cassette)
Jerome K. Jerome: *Three Men in a Boat* Read by Jeremy Nicholas
ARGO SAY 86 (double cassette)

B Use of radio

'Morning Story' is a good source of stories for listening practice and hearing good
reading in practice. It is broadcast every weekday morning at 10.30 a.m. on Radio 4
and lasts for fifteen minutes. Older students might be encouraged to listen to this
during holidays and free time. There are also many Radio 4 programmes concerned
with putting across points of view. Listening to some of these can be excellent
practice for many aspects of oral work: 'Any Questions?'; 'Any Answers?'; 'Woman's
Hour'; 'Start the Week'; 'Stop the Week'; 'The World at One'; 'The World Tonight'.

Students should also try to take an intelligent interest in the many excellent
discussion programmes on television.

Suggested answers

Talking

Page 18—How do I make an omelette?

What was wrong?

a) Anyone asking the question is clearly not an experienced cook! The instruction, 'Break the egg', suggests smashing the egg with a hammer. It makes no mention of throwing away the shell!

b) 'Add some milk, salt and pepper.' How much? Could end up very salty, so peppery you can't eat it for sneezing and so milky it's like a drink with an egg in it—or with too little it could be tasteless and tiny.

c) Put 'it' in a basin. What's 'it'?—looks as if the shell's going in again. Very tasty!

d) Surely the egg would have gone into the basin before the salt, pepper and milk were added? Pretty messy otherwise!

e) 'Beat well.' What does that mean?

f) 'Turn into a frying pan.'
'No, I'd rather be a toad.'—It sounds like an instruction from a wizard.

g) 'Heat it.' Ouch! I can feel the blazing flames and smell the burning pan already.

h) How do I slide it? It's likely to end up on the floor unless I'm told *how* to get it out of the pan.

How to make an omelette–suggested instructions

1   Take two eggs for each person. Break them one at a time by sharply tapping the centre of each with a knife. Empty the inside of the egg into a cup and throw away the shell. Then tip the egg into a large basin. Break the eggs in this way so that if there is a bad one, it does not ruin the others.

2   Add a level teaspoon of salt to every six eggs and half that amount of pepper. To make the mixture go further, you can add up to a sixth of a pint of milk for every two eggs.

3   Take a fork and mix the milk and eggs together by a fast to and fro movement (called 'beating'). Carry on until the eggs and milk have combined to form a pale yellow liquid.

4   Heat just enough butter or margarine to cover the bottom of the frying pan. Use a very low heat or the butter will burn. Put droplets of the omelette mix into the fat one at a time, every few seconds. As soon as a droplet sizzles, the fat is hot enough. Pour the mixture into the pan, still over a very low heat.

5   A skin will form quickly on the underside. Keep lifting the side of this skin with a spatula so that the liquid runs under the skin and gets cooked.

6   The omelette is cooked as soon as the centre has lost its wet look.

7   Use the spatula to fold the omelette in half. Slide the spatula underneath to ensure that the omelette is not stuck to the pan. Then take the pan to the plate and carefully ease the omelette from the pan to the plate, using the spatula to help you.

Note: It is always helpful in giving instructions to explain WHY something is being done. It's easier to remember if it makes sense.

Page 19—How to clean your teeth

a) Think through exactly what you do.
b) From this, make notes of sequence:
    Holding brush—toothpaste—brushing—all surfaces—rinse brush—toothpaste lid.
c) 'Speech' from notes:
    Take the lid off the toothpaste. Hold the brush by the handle (not the end with bristles!) Moisten the brush under running cold water. Take the toothpaste tube in your other hand and squeeze a strip of toothpaste to cover the top of the bristles. Open mouth slightly and lift lips back by their own muscles. Place bristles against the top front teeth. Move the brush from side to side several times over the front teeth, holding the brush at an angle of 45° to the teeth. Then move to the left a tooth at a time until you've reached the extreme left end. Take care over the very last teeth which may be awkward—but not impossible—to reach. Then go back to the centre and repeat to the right. This will require you to turn the toothbrush round the other way! When you have reached the extreme right, repeat the process for the bottom teeth. Then pay attention to the upper surfaces of the teeth and finally do your best to clean the surfaces behind the teeth.
    Finally rinse carefully, wash the toothbrush—and don't forget to put the lid back on the toothpaste.

Reading

Page 52—Cheese

a) 'The smell of the cheese. He was probably trying to run away from it!' (*Short answer—but not surly. Still conversational, in response to tone of question*).

b) 'I don't like cheese at all, so to me they sound awful. I think I'd react more like the horse. But they *are* described in a way that makes you feel how delicious they were to the writer.'

or

'Yes. I really like strong cheeses—in fact strong-tasting food of any kind. I think that bit about the two-hundred horse-power scent really brings out what people like about good strong cheese.'

(*Longer answers—showing that you are a person, not a machine!*)

c) 'Well, there's the description of the cheeses, which makes them sound very powerful. Then the repeated "With pleasure" makes you know something nasty's coming! When you get to the horse he's so much weaker than the cheese and I liked that sarcastic phrase about "a moment of enthusiasm". The comparisons are funny too—"the swiftest steam-roller ever built", and I like the contradiction of "dashing off" and *three* miles per hour. It's also a good comic picture of the three humans holding back this worn-out but determined old horse.'

(*Longish answer, showing that you can think about the reading and see how the writer is working. Some of this would probably come out with stops and starts as you suddenly notice things—that's all right and quite natural in speech.*)

Page 53—Willy

1 'He unbolts the door.'

(*Simple answer to a factual, closed question. Understanding tested. An 'easy' question is often used to relax nervous candidates. Once you've got something right, you usually feel better.*)

2 'She was probably worried about him playing with the other children. She might have thought they'd bully him, but I think probably she didn't want him to be involved in their fighting and swearing.'

(*Longer answer, needing some point of view. Q.3 could well arise from your answer here: the examiner doesn't necessarily have a set list of questions.*)

3 (*No right or wrong answers! What's wanted is a* point of view.)

'I wouldn't have kept him away from the others. It only makes them laugh at him and think he's a baby. You've got to learn to live with other people: it's no use trying to keep children in cotton wool. When Willy grows up he'll probably rebel against his mum and get into more trouble than the street kids.'

4 (*Again a check on understanding, rather than response, though you can develop it beyond the passage—it's not a written comprehension paper.*)

'Oh, they think he's posh and molly-coddled, so they poke fun at his nice clothes, his rather strict father—he sounds a bit old-fashioned—and his fussy mum. They think he's still treated like a toddler: aren't reins the things you put on young children to stop them falling over?'

5 (*Open question for interpretation.*)

He sounds like a school teacher, with a cane, perhaps the headmaster of the local junior school. Or he could just be a tall, thin, rather frightening neighbour—after all, to young children tall people look *very* tall!

Listening

Page 56—'The Wind and the Sun'

Aesop's moral is 'Persuasion often succeeds where force fails'. **B** may work out something like this, though he/she may simply conclude that heat is harder to endure than cold.

Page 57—'Belling the Cat'

Aesop's moral here, for **A** to work out, is that 'things are easier said than done'.

Page 57—'His eyes scrutinized . . .'

He has tried to escape from a village by climbing up a mountain, but has fallen.

Page 58—*Billy Liar*

A scruffy place. The Moor has been taken over by the cast-offs of the town. Depressing.

Page 59—*Saturday Night and Sunday Morning*

Noisy, jarring, discordant. The machines have driven out the man's natural life—note that it's important to get the point of the fishing reference.

Page 59—*The Food of the Gods*

The answer must take account of the last sentence.

Pages 60–3—Argument

a) George Orwell: *The Road to Wigan Pier*
   Main idea: All human activity is dependent on coal mining, yet we rarely think about it.

   Particular ideas:
   Remoteness of coal mining from most people's lives.
   People's indifference.
   Coal needed in peace and war.
   Connection between home usage and mining.
   Miners' work essential to modern life.

b) Department of Transport: *Driving*
   Main idea: The driver's attitude.

   Particular ideas:
   Things learned by experience and things needed from the start.
   Safety, concentration, patience and courtesy.
   Need to develop these qualities from the start.
   Very difficult for some people.
   Even experienced drivers need a good attitude.

c) Alison Edwards: *She*
   Main idea: Get rid of parents' evenings.

   Particular ideas:
   Unprofitable for parents, teachers and children.
   Pupils not delivering notes.
   The wrong parents attend.
   Irritations of waiting.
   Predictability of what is said.
   Cause rows and resentment.
   More accurate methods of assessment.

Reading passage for page 65

At a very early age Lydia Kemeny learned not to put down roots. Her father often told her: 'You can live anywhere' and the child accepted the statement and was unsurprised when life proved it to be true.

She was born in Vienna in Austria, the ony child of a Hungarian artist father and a Czech mother, and when she was two the family returned to her mother's home town, Pilsen. But by 1938 her father, frustrated by his artistic isolation, had decided that France was the place for an artist to live.

First, however, he set off on a trip through Belgium and Holland to paint, visit the galleries and pay a visit to his cousins in Britain. His cousins insisted that safety could only be found this side of the channel.

'I think my father was a little shocked,' says Lydia, now 52 and head of a fashion department at a college of art in London. 'You see, although hatred and suspicion of the Germans was traditional in Czechoslovakia, there was no real sense of approaching disaster; only outside the country, you could see it clearly.'

Mr Kemeny sent for his wife and daughter and the Czech authorities granted then exit permits to go to Britain. But his wife was reluctant to leave her parents and her home. She procrastinated, dragging out the packing and the arrangements for moving. And Hitler's troops marched into Czechoslovakia.

The Germans established their occupation very quickly and all exit permits were cancelled. 'My mother and I had to apply for new permits. I remember we were so frightened. But they had to grant them because we held Hungarian passports and Hungary was an ally. There was a complete embargo on Czech nationals.'

So 12-year old Lydia and her mother took the train across Europe. It was a terrifying journey and Lydia cultivated a calm and confident manner to reassure her anxious mother.

Her father had taken a small furnished flat in Maida Vale in London while he looked for a permanent home and Lydia was sent to a boarding school nearby. 'I could speak Latin better than I could speak English and, although everyone was very kind I appeared in the first weeks to take in nothing at all. Then, before the end of my first term, I caught scarlet fever and they carted me off to a children's isolation hospital.

'There were about 20 children and a Brown Owl, Girl Guide Leader, who had caught something nasty off one of her Brownies. She must have been God's gift to that hospital because she organized games and kept us busy and—what was quite extraordinary—I emerged six weeks later speaking fluent English.'

For Lydia the war years were a protracted battle of wills between herself and her mother over whether she could be billeted safely in the country or stay in London. Most of the time Lydia lost. She lodged with many different kinds of people in country towns in the Home Counties and was only unhappy once—with a lady of 70 who did not understand 14-year-olds.

'No one ever made me feel a stranger or a foreigner. Sometimes I overheard remarks like: "Bloody foreigners" but they were never directed at me and I was never offended by them. You see right from the start, I identified totally with England. It is only now, so many years later, that I realize that my adaptability was perhaps unusual. But I had had to accept change as part of my life very early on.'

It was also a matter of temperament. 'I think I was a victim of smother love which meant I had to be tough to assert my own identity, but I had also developed, by the time I reached Britain, some very British attitudes as a way of coping with an anxious emotional mother.'

Since she thinks in English and feels thoroughly British, Lydia was surprised a few years back to realize that the scenes she paints and which she thought wholly the product of her imagination, are in fact rather idealized memories of the Czechoslovakian countryside.

'One thing I have which I know is attributable to my Czech heritage is a strong sense of the decorative in design. I delight in rich, decorative borders like those you see on peasant costumes or furniture.'

Lydia, who is married to an architect, has two children, Tania, who is 25 and Martin, 22. Tania revels in her Central European ancestry and still begs her grandmother for old folk tales and memories of the old country. 'Martin, however,' says Lydia, 'finds it regrettable that he is not totally English. Maybe it won't always be that way. Maybe one day he will realize that his origins do not detract from his identity as an Englishman. They just add an extra, rich dimension.'

(*The Guardian*, 6 September 1979)

Page 65—Questions

1   a) Lydia was twelve when she came to Britain.
     b) Her husband is an architect.

2   Her father decided that he and his family should leave Czechoslovakia to obtain greater artistic freedom and avoid the impending invasion.

3   They had Hungarian passports because Lydia's father was Hungarian.

4   The advantage of possessing Hungarian passports was that the Germans had placed an embargo on the exit permits of Czech nationals.

5   Mrs Kemeny was anxious, emotional and over-protective towards Lydia. (*You could replace any one of these by the idea that she was deeply attached to her country*).

6   Lydia came to speak English fluently after spending six weeks in a hospital with 20 children and a Girl Guide Leader who kept them busy with games.

7   Lydia thinks she was able to settle happily and quickly in Britain because of her positive temperament. Also, she was used to change.

8   Lydia's Czech childhood influenced her life as an artist in landscape painting (*or*: design).

9   (*Example*) Lydia's background had made her adaptable, independent, confident, aware of the importance of tradition and appreciative of the richness of a multi-cultural background.

Reading passage for page 66

And so Willy ran away again. But this second time it was not adventure, but rage and shame that drove him out. He felt he would never be able to hold his head up again, never be able to face school, after what his father had said to the schoolmaster. He ran out into the passage, slamming the parlour door behind him so that the house rocked, and stormed down towards the back door.

'There's some chips here for you,' called his mother faintly from the kitchen. 'I'm keeping them hot.'

'I'm not hungry,' he shouted back, and burst out, down the steps into the yard. But the yard was too small to hold him in the violence of his despair. Clenching and unclenching his hands he stood there, looking wildly round him. He wanted to do something destructive, something that would hurt. But the whitewashed walls of the yard held nothing except the dustbin and the sheeted form of the tandem. On an impulse he strode over to this and tore its covers from it, and stood glaring at it. He wanted to kick down the house, kick down Audley Street and the Northern Star, and trample noisily on the ruins. Instead, he took the tandem and the wheel of events that had taken charge of him when he was six whirled him on the second great adventure of his life.

He did not really come to his senses until he had got to the top of the hill down into Stockport. He must have cycled five or six miles almost without noticing it in his mad fury. But by the time he could see the chimneys and the smoke of Stockport, and the huge viaduct that spanned the valley, the frenzied energy that had seized and swept him so far was leaving him, and he was for the first time aware of how heavy the machine was and how difficult to control. But now it was plunging down the hill and it was too late for commonsense to reassert itself. As he lurched and jolted over the cobblestones, clinging to the brown handlegrips, he wondered if he had the strength to keep all that weight of iron on the road and himself on the saddle. It was in fact the first rational thought he had had since he stormed out of the parlour.

He did reach the bottom safely, but only by narrowly missing a couple of trams and grazing a brewer's dray, whose driver cursed him and flicked at him with his whip. And then he dismounted and stood by the kerb, wiping his coat sleeve over his forehead, his knees shaking so much that he wanted to sit down. A lot of people gave him and his machine curious glances, but Willy hardly cared.

He was roused by a wailing howl that he ought to have known well enough, since he heard it day and night at home—the sound of a factory buzzer. Out of a yard down a side street came the clatter of hundreds of feet, and within a moment or two the workers had appeared, girls with their shawls drawn over their heads and mobs of men. Shouting, laughing and chattering, they swirled round Willy while he clutched defensively at the handlebars of his machine. It attracted enough attention from the men. They clustered around, commenting upon it, addressing remarks to each other and to Willy which he was too bewildered to hear.

'Well, aren't you going to give us an answer?' somebody bawled into his ear.

'What do you mean?' said Willy apprehensively.

'We wants a ride.'

'You're a fine one. Got two seats and won't give a ride.'

'It isn't mine.'

'Hear that? He's nicked it. Nicked a bike for two. Did you ever hear the like! And won't let honest folk use it. Come on lads, get it from him.' And a thick-set, red-faced youth laid his hands on the back handlebars.

'No!' shouted Willy, scarlet with anger. 'You keep your hands off it, it's my father's.'

'Let him alone,' put in another voice, 'he's only a little lad. They don't mean no harm,' it went on reassuringly. 'Don't you go crying.'

'I'm not crying,' said Willy furiously, though tears of anger were standing in his eyes.

The crowd was melting away now, its interest dwindling, and Willy was left with only two of the mill hands. 'They don't mean no harm,' repeated his protector. 'They will have their bit of fun. Where is you dad, then?'

'In Ardwick.'

'Ardwick? Where do you come from then?'

Willy liked the look of him. He had fresh red cheeks, and bright blue merry eyes. 'I come from Ardwick,' he said, relaxing a little.

'What, rid from Ardwick all on your lonesome?'

Willy nodded.

'Well, you've got strength for such a spindleshanks. Are you going to take it all the way back then?'

'I suppose so,' said Willy doubtfully. He had not started to think about his return.

'Why, you'll never get it there, a little lad like you. Will he, Jack?' The youth turned to his companion, a lanky pale boy, with a long, solemn face. Jack shook his head gloomily.

'Nay, that he won't. Up this hill?' He sucked in his breath and pursed his lips. 'Oh no, that's not for little lads like him.'

'You see what Jack says. You'll never get it there. Where do you live?'

'19, Audley Street,' faltered Willy, beginning to feel miserably doubtful about those bright blue eyes which seemed to be having a secret joke with the other youth.

'And where's 19, Audley Street when it's at home?'

'It's my father's shop, Audley Street is near Grosvenor Street.'

'Well, I'll tell you what we'll do, Jack and me, seeing as we're the kindly sort. We'll ride it back to Audley Street for you and hand it over to your dad. It'll get back safer that way, eh Jack?' He winked heavily at his companion. 'Now Jack, you swing that leg of yours over the back seat and I'll take the front. And you stand away, young'un, if you don't want to be rid down.'

Dumbly, Willy stood back and watched the machine wobble across the road, down a side street and disappear. Then he came to his senses.

'Stop!' he screamed, and plunged across in pursuit, under the noses of a pair of tram horses. He dodged away from their feet, dimly hearing the driver shouting at him. There was no sign of the tandem down the side street. He went all the way down it, thrusting through the groups of shawled women, the children sprawled on the pavements, and then made his way back to the main street. Perhaps it was all a joke, perhaps they would be bringing it back. He took up his post at the point where he had last seen them and scanned the road, turning his head anxiously to keep a watch in both directions.

Page 67—Questions

1　He is full of anger and embarrassment. He feels very destructive and wants to get his own back on his father.

2　We know that Willy looked young because the men from the factory say he's only a little lad. He behaved childishly by acting without thinking and by being taken in by the youth's trick.

3　The mill hand who stands up for Willy seems very kind and protective. Willy likes the look of his red cheeks and blue eyes. He seems to be trying to help Willy.

4　Willy begins to be suspicious when he starts to feel that the youths are secretly laughing at him.

5　Willy only comes to his senses when the tandem is ridden out of sight.

6　Willy would want to think it was a joke because he doesn't want the tandem to be stolen or to get into more trouble with his father. He probably doesn't like feeling a fool either.

(*Tip: look at the number of marks for each question. Make sure you've said enough to get the marks.*)